# Connecting the Dots in World History, A Teacher's Literacy-Based Curriculum

# Connecting the Dots in World History, A Teacher's Literacy-Based Curriculum

## From Human Origins to Constantine

VOLUME I

Chris Edwards, EdD

*Rowman & Littlefield*
Lanham • Boulder • New York • London

Published by Rowman & Littlefield
A wholly owned subsidiary of The Rowman & Littlefield Publishing Group, Inc.
4501 Forbes Boulevard, Suite 200, Lanham, Maryland 20706
www.rowman.com

Unit A, Whitacre Mews, 26-34 Stannary Street, London SE11 4AB

Copyright © 2015 by Chris Edwards

*All rights reserved.* No part of this book may be reproduced in any form or by any electronic or mechanical means, including information storage and retrieval systems, without written permission from the publisher, except by a reviewer who may quote passages in a review.

British Library Cataloguing in Publication Information Available

**Library of Congress Cataloging-in-Publication Data**

Edwards, Chris, 1977–
 Connecting the dots in world history, a teacher's literacy-based curriculum / Chris Edwards, EdD.
  volumes cm
 Includes bibliographical references.
 Contents: Volume 1. From human origins to Constantine — Volume 2. From the Fall of the Western Roman Empire to Death of Genghis Khan — Volume 3. From the Mongol Empire to the Reformation — Volume 4. From the Reformation to the Beginning of the Collapse of the Ottoman Empire — Volume 5. From the Napoleonic Era to the Collapse of the Soviet Union.
  ISBN 978-1-4758-2144-4 (v. 1 : cloth : alk. paper) — ISBN 978-1-4758-2145-1 (v. 1 : pbk. : alk. paper) — ISBN 978-1-4758-2146-8 (v. 1 : electronic) — ISBN 978-1-4758-2314-1 (v. 2 : cloth : alk. paper) — ISBN 978-1-4758-2315-8 (v. 2 : pbk. : alk. paper) — ISBN 978-1-4758-2316-5 (v. 2 : electronic) — ISBN 978-1-4758-2317-2 (v. 3 : cloth : alk. paper) — ISBN 978-1-4758-2318-9 (v. 3 : pbk. : alk. paper) — ISBN 978-1-4758-2319-6 (v. 3 : electronic) — ISBN 978-1-4758-2341-7 (v. 4 : cloth : alk. paper) — ISBN 978-1-4758-2342-4 (v. 4 : pbk. : alk. paper) — ISBN 978-1-4758-2343-1 (v. 4 : electronic) — ISBN 978-1-4758-2344-8 (v. 5 : cloth : alk. paper) — ISBN 978-1-4758-2345-5 (v. 5 : pbk. : alk. paper) — ISBN 978-1-4758-2346-2 (v. 5 : electronic) 1. History—Study and teaching—United States. 2. Curriculum planning—United States. I. Title.
 D16.3.E43 2015
 907.1—dc23                                                    2015022437

∞™ The paper used in this publication meets the minimum requirements of American National Standard for Information Sciences—Permanence of Paper for Printed Library Materials, ANSI/NISO Z39.48-1992.

Printed in the United States of America

*This has always been for my students.*

# CONTENTS

Preface . . . . . . . . . . . . . . . . . . . . . . . . . . . . . . . . . . . . . . . . . . . . . . ix
Acknowledgments . . . . . . . . . . . . . . . . . . . . . . . . . . . . . . . . . . . xvii
Introduction . . . . . . . . . . . . . . . . . . . . . . . . . . . . . . . . . . . . . . . . 1
**CHAPTER ONE**  Human Migrations . . . . . . . . . . . . . . . . . . . . . . . . . 7
**CHAPTER TWO**  The Dots Form . . . . . . . . . . . . . . . . . . . . . . . . . . 17
**CHAPTER THREE**  Greece . . . . . . . . . . . . . . . . . . . . . . . . . . . . . . 27
**CHAPTER FOUR**  The Wars . . . . . . . . . . . . . . . . . . . . . . . . . . . . . 37
**CHAPTER FIVE**  Greek Philosophy . . . . . . . . . . . . . . . . . . . . . . . . . 49
**CHAPTER SIX**  Alexander's Era . . . . . . . . . . . . . . . . . . . . . . . . . . 61
**CHAPTER SEVEN**  Rome . . . . . . . . . . . . . . . . . . . . . . . . . . . . . . 73
**CHAPTER EIGHT**  The Han . . . . . . . . . . . . . . . . . . . . . . . . . . . . 85
**CHAPTER NINE**  From Republic to Empire in Rome . . . . . . . . . . . . 95
**CHAPTER TEN**  After Caesar . . . . . . . . . . . . . . . . . . . . . . . . . . . 109
**CHAPTER ELEVEN**  Judaism, Christianity, and Constantine . . . . . . . . 121
Appendix . . . . . . . . . . . . . . . . . . . . . . . . . . . . . . . . . . . . . . . . 135
References . . . . . . . . . . . . . . . . . . . . . . . . . . . . . . . . . . . . . . . 145
About the Author . . . . . . . . . . . . . . . . . . . . . . . . . . . . . . . . . . 149

# PREFACE

*Obsessed with upholding the family honor, he cannot embrace the title of sculptor or painter, which he associates with degraded manual labor. . . . Driven to become an artist, a profession he knew was beneath his dignity, Michelangelo simply redefined the term.*

—Miles Unger, *Michelangelo: A Life in Six Masterpieces*

*If we accept the limitations of our decentralized political system, we can move towards a future in which sustainable and transformative education reforms are seeded from the ground up, not imposed from the top down. They will be built more upon the expertise of the best teachers than on our fears of the worst teachers.*

—Dana Goldstein, *The Teacher Wars: A History of America's Most Embattled Profession*

Textbooks are compiled, not written. This curriculum differs from a textbook in that it was crafted to align with learning theory. Where textbooks simply present block after block of information, occasionally complemented by colorful graphs and bold words, this curriculum presents a narrative.

Research into educational practice indicates that people learn when information is presented in a narrative format, and so this curriculum was designed with that concept in mind. I first began writing my own materials for the classroom when I realized that the textbooks I was given simply did not fit with what educational research indicated was best practice for actually educating students.

In order to correct this disjunction between educational practice and the tools I was given to use as a teacher, I began the process of compiling information into a format that fit with learning theory. I teach world history and Advanced Placement world history now, but back when I taught eighth grade U.S. history, I began implementing this new philosophy. The curriculum I made was developed around a "connect-the-dots" metaphor.

A connect-the-dots game begins when a person is given a seemingly random series of dots but then, upon instruction, connects those dots to see a bigger picture. The brain is complex and defies any easy attempt at explanation, but long-standing findings in neuroscience indicate that information is stored and strengthened in the brain through its connections to other pieces of information. (Think of how a conversation between two people can wind all over the place as each conversant makes a novel connection that then causes another conversant to make a separate connection, etc.) A good curriculum should present information in a way that is in alignment with this principle.

In 2008, the National Council for Social Studies published a paper I had written: "Connecting-the-Dots: Making Meaning from Historical Evidence." This paper detailed the method I had created by showing how I had taken the ideas presented in Jared Diamond's *Guns, Germs, and Steel* and made them relevant to my eighth-grade history students in a way that aligned with educational best practices.

Creating these kinds of lessons was intellectually demanding, as I had to master the historical content before I could develop a way to make that content accessible to students, but once I saw how well these types of lessons could work in class, nothing else was acceptable. I started compiling lesson after lesson until I had a year's worth. About that time, I took a job teaching world history. This is the biggest topic there is, and I wanted to continue on using my method despite the overwhelming nature of the content.

It took me over seven years of study, writing, and editing, but this curriculum is the product of that long period of labor. Here is the entire history of the world put into a format that is in alignment with educational best practices and the Common Core reading and writing philosophy.

# PREFACE

This was originally created for my students, but there are several reasons why I wanted to seek publication, and these should be stated here.

The first reason I sought to publish my curriculum was because in my first book with Rowman & Littlefield, titled *Teaching Genius: Redefining Education with Lessons from Science and Philosophy*, I expanded on an argument I had made in an earlier paper that was published in the science and philosophy journal *Skeptic*. The argument I made in the book and the paper is that teaching should be defined as a field that is separate from both the content-area field and the field of education but comprises elements of each. Practitioners in the field of teaching would then create a "product"—not the product of research but a synthesis of method and content. Let's simply call that product a curriculum.

Under this definition of teaching as a field, teachers would constantly study their content for personal understanding and then develop ways to make that content accessible to their students using best practices in education. I wanted to publish this curriculum to show what a completely teacher-generated curriculum can look like. Law, medicine, psychology, history, mathematics, physics, and so forth all have their great canons of works, but teaching does not. It's time that changed.

The second reason I sought publication was that, starting around 2006 with the publication of solid research by Tom Kane, Robert Gordon, and Douglas Staiger, it became apparent to educational researchers that the only school-based factor that could significantly improve student performance was the individual teacher. Furthermore, it was found that the level of degree attained by the teacher had no measurable impact on his or her classroom efficacy. Independent research corroborated these findings.

This new evidence led to a series of flawed "reform" efforts that took away the monetary awards given to teachers for accruing degrees. The findings by Kane, Gordon, and Staiger should have instead led to a massive overhaul of the teacher training system in the United States. Teachers are, in general, trained to study content in part of the university and methods in another part of the university; they are never given specific training on how to combine the two into a curriculum.

Let me ask this uncomfortable question: Why should the work that teachers do to attain degrees and the work that teachers do to create curricula be separate from one another? In fact, most of us who have completed master's and doctoral work will probably state that the work we did to attain our degrees acted as a distraction from the everyday work of creating a curriculum for teaching. Shouldn't the work that teachers do in graduate school actually enhance what happens in their classrooms?

By defining teaching as a separate field, this is what would occur. This published curriculum should not just serve as the first book in the canon of teacher curricula but also be seen as an example of what a doctoral dissertation in the field of teaching might look like. Teacher training should enhance the classroom experience for the students of the teachers. Teachers should have to present truly great curricula, not research-based dissertations, in order to attain degrees.

Those who want to research educational policy and educational methods can stay in the field of education, but let those who want to teach actually work and study in the field of teaching.

The third reason I sought publication was to demonstrate that a new form of analysis and critical thinking that I have been practicing can in fact be taught. It has always seemed to me that if the purpose of education is to teach people how to think critically, then it should be the case that individuals with an educational theory should have proved their own ability to think critically before telling others how it can be done.

I'll apply this standard to myself. I offer here a book that is designed to increase a student's content-area knowledge and cognitive capacities, and so I should be able to prove that my methods actually work in various intellectual arenas. I have done this. I say this not to brag, but rather to present my credentials and to prove a point.

In the last several years, *Skeptic* magazine, which is a science and philosophy journal that features many of the Western world's most important intellectuals (including Michael Shermer, Jared Diamond, Harriet Myers, and the physicist/science historian John Gribbin) on its editorial board, has published half a dozen of my papers. In those papers, I have engaged with the best minds of the last century over matters of philosophy, metaphysics, and epistemology, and I have gone right to the heart of theoretical physics. I've uncovered the fallacies inherent in books of the philosopher Robert Pirsig and the inventor/physicist Ray Kurzweil. I've challenged the theoretical position of Model Dependent Realism espoused by Stephen Hawking and Leonard Mlodinow, as well the concept of "Moral Cognition Testing," which is a core feature of the psychology departments at both Princeton and Harvard. I wrote a long piece explaining the historical significance of Douglas Hofstadter's position on how analogical thinking is at the cognitive center of all scientific endeavors.

All of this work has been peer reviewed and published. In my recent book *Novum Organum II: Going Beyond the Scientific Research Model* (2014), I devoted an entire chapter to rethinking relativity theory given the new epistemological positions I have been writing on. An intellectual revolution has been occurring that can only be considered analogous to the Scientific Revolution. This revolution requires new types of thinking that can be taught.

The aforementioned papers demonstrate my personal ability to think critically, and my educational work connects classroom practice to that endeavor. Sometimes, after I've given a talk to members of the philosophical or scientific community, I am told that I'm overqualified to be a teacher. Nothing could be less truthful. I'm not overqualified; teaching is undervalued.

Whatever critical thinking skills I possess, I owe them to being a practitioner in the field of teaching. Since I publish widely in the fields that require critical thinking, I feel qualified to say that I have something to say about how critical thinking can be taught. This curriculum is intended to develop a new concept of teaching for teachers and a new era of cognition for students.

This may sound immodest, but it brings us to the fourth and final reason I wanted publish this curriculum: Teachers must claim the momentum for educational reform; we cannot be passive or, worse, passive aggressive. Teachers still control the daily classroom experience and still have quite a lot of individual authority when it comes to tailoring lessons and leading students. We cannot be intimidated or exhausted by the bureaucracy.

One of the most disturbing trends I've seen coming from educators has been the "We'll bleed until somebody helps us" mentality. This can be seen in a variety of educational materials, many of them put out by unions, which offer stories of good teachers who have left the profession out of frustration with the "system."

The "system" has always been a mess and always will be. Our focus should be on the creation of curriculum in the field of teaching. By way of example, let's look at Michelangelo, the sculptor of the statue of David and the painter of the Sistine Chapel. He, too, had to deal with small-minded bureaucrats and engage in petty-minded squabbles over money and deadlines. The great artist also obsessed over his best creative work in an era when painting and sculpting suffered from low status. It would be a mistake to think that Michelangelo created his works of artistic genius despite these political and societal constraints. In fact, these factors *drove* Michelangelo. Through the sheer force of his obsessive genius, Michelangelo raised the status of the sculptor and the painter. Nobody remembers the bureaucrats and politicians who were ostensibly above Michelangelo in rank. But everyone knows Michelangelo because he created something new, something original, something that no one else could even conceive.

I suspect that the great artist was driven by more than just a desire to create beauty; something must have existed in his ego that forced him to work for numerous unsleeping hours. The great reward must have come when the covers came off of David, and all the squabbling penny pinchers who had bothered him about deadlines and who wanted him to just do as he was told had to stand there and look at the marvel of Michelangelo's creation.

Michelangelo must have been thinking *you can't do this*. Of course, I'm not intending to compare my curriculum to any of Michelangelo's creations. However, it is important for teachers, who are so used to telling students "You *can* do this," to realize that it is sometimes necessary to announce to people outside of the classroom, through the sheer force of creating products in our field, *you can't do this*. Or, at least, you can't do this without years of proper education and training.

Teaching requires the same kind of specialized and refined skills as sculpting, and I, as a teacher, am not intimidated by the "reformers." Instead, I am motivated to show that teachers can be bigger than the system and that the system will therefore change to accommodate us. Show me the Teach For America participant who can create a curriculum of this quality in just two years, and I'll never write another word about education.

Teachers, *we* will change education. We do not need to wait for anyone else. We do not need to wait for systemic change. We do not need to wait to be paid more. We do not need to wait for respect. We can synthesize method with content and *create*. Everything else will follow. Do not cede power to those outside the classroom. You paint your Sistine Chapel and make the bureaucrats feel small when they have to look up. Systemic reform begins in your mind and in your classroom.

# PREFACE

I am a practitioner in the most intellectually challenging field on the planet: teaching. I'd like to invite other teachers to join me in this new field, and I hope this curriculum provides inspiration and that this inspiration benefits students.

## Note to Teachers

New literacy standards, including the Common Core, are animated by a philosophy requiring that content be transmitted to students primarily through reading, and assessments are designed to test the reading and critical thinking skills of students. The text of this volume is in alignment with Common Core standards and with other literacy standards based around this reading theory. Rather than clunk up the text with assessments and assignments, a few samples (including a final assessment) are included in the appendix, along with explanations.

The books in the "Connecting the Dots" series are not textbooks and therefore do not need to be vetted by a textbook committee should a teacher choose to use these books or parts of them in class. Please feel free to use these books as a classroom resource insofar as your standards and laws on copyright allow.

Please do also note that this is a curriculum, something intended to be read and analyzed by students for the purpose of preparing secondary students for the assessments generated here. These books are not intended as works of scholarship. (Susan Wise Bauer is currently three volumes into what I believe will be the definitive work of world history for generations; she is creating a work of scholarly genius, and I do not wish to be compared to her!)

# ACKNOWLEDGMENTS

I would like to say thanks to a number of people for their support of this lengthy project. Tom Koerner is a wonderful editor who has always been willing to take a chance on my books. Thanks also to Christine Fahey for her communication and assistance. Patricia Stevenson provided invaluable advice in both grammar and content, and I am especially grateful for both. Thanks likewise go to Charlie Guthrie for his editorial advice and inspiring conversation. I'd like to thank the Indianapolis-based Scientech Foundation for supporting many of my ideas for educational reform through their generous funding of the Scientech Summer Institute for math and science teachers. In addition, I'd like to thank Jason Urban and Valerie Piehl for supporting the in-class dimensions of this project. My wife, Beth, deserves special thanks for hardly ever interrupting me while I'm working. My sons, Blake and Ben, almost always interrupt me when I'm working, and for that they deserve more than a thank-you.

# INTRODUCTION

In 1861, the first year of the American Civil War, the most common rifle used by soldiers was loaded through the barrel and could shoot accurately for up to one hundred yards. By 1945, the United States dropped two atom bombs on Japan. A sixteen-year-old soldier fighting in the first year of the Civil War could have conceivably lived to see his country drop those atomic bombs if he reached the age of one hundred.

On December 17, 1903, a homemade flying machine, built by two bicycle repairmen named Orville and Wilbur Wright, and containing a propeller and engine, made a rickety flight along the beach in Kitty Hawk, North Carolina. Sixty-six years later, on July 20, 1969, NASA astronauts walked on the moon. Someone who was ten years old at the time of the first machine-produced flight would only have been seventy-six when the moon landing occurred.

Depending on how one defines the term, gunpowder weapons have been around since the early thirteenth century; yet between the thirteenth and nineteenth centuries they made only meager progress. Weapons evolved from bombasts to cannons, and then to muskets and handguns, followed by repeating rifles, then rockets, and eventually atomic bombs.

For most of human history, humans lacked any flight capacity at all. Except for the few and deeply unfortunate individuals who were shot from catapults, all humans were confined to the ground. By the late eighteenth century, helium balloons allowed for a few people in France to take flight, but mechanical flight did not exist until 1903. Then humans were on the moon within just a few decades.

INTRODUCTION

These are arbitrary examples of the rate of technological change, chosen only because they represent some of the most recognizable historical events of the nineteenth and twentieth centuries, but the rapid development in the areas of ballistics and flight (tied together though they were) does raise some questions. For instances, why did weapons technology and flight technology both evolve so rapidly in a short period of time, only to then level off once a certain level had been reached?

These questions have answers: Technology and ideas evolve when combined with one another, and sometimes a certain level of complexity has to be reached through a slow and herky-jerky historical process before people can see a pattern and formalize a previously random historical process. For example, in the biological sphere it can take millions of years for an animal to evolve a new trait through the random process of natural selection. However, when human breeders directly control the passing on of genetic characteristics through purposeful breeding, traits can evolve quickly.

Technology stops evolving at a rapid rate because development comes with an energy cost. As rockets get sent further and further into space, the price tag hanging on the end of them gets larger. Spending money on weapons technology raises ethical questions, and, once a country possesses enough weapons to end civilization on Earth, it seems frivolous to develop weapons that could end potentially nonexistent alien civilizations.

One could even argue that the examples presented here are misplaced. The landing of a space shuttle on the moon might be better categorized as being in the field of ballistics rather than flight. The astronauts were riding in rockets, after all. NASA's moon landing might be more closely connected with a Civil War rifle than it is with the plane the Wright brothers built. The atom bombs were dropped, not launched, after all, while the NASA space shuttle incorporated the same kind of rocket technology that launched missiles in the Second World War.

Technological evolution, like biological evolution, creates a tangle of connections. Sometimes the dots in a connect-the-dots game can make different pictures depending upon how one draws the lines together.

Alfred Crosby, Jared Diamond, and Peter Watson have completed some fascinating scholarly work about the impact of geography on the development of civilization (although the use of geography as a historical explanatory tool reaches back to the Enlightenment). Rather than give a dry analysis of each scholar's books, it's best to just synthesize their general ideas under a single explanation.

It's possible to view world history as a global experiment regarding the impacts of geography. We could think of the supercontinent of Eurasia as a single "petri dish" for humanity, viewing the Americas, Africa, and the various islands of the South Pacific as separate petri dishes. Up until 1492, people living in Eurasia might have asked, "What would happen if human civilization was wiped out and forced to start again in a different geographic environment?" After 1492, when a vast population of humans was found living in North and South America, this question would have been rhetorical. We now have real answers.

Jared Diamond has written that the geography of Eurasia, and particularly a single region in the Middle East known as the Fertile Crescent, proved to be the most favorable for the development of cities. To explain this concept, known as geographic determinism, imagine a scenario where someone from California or Hawaii derides the citizens of the state of Indiana for not having better surfers. The citizens of Indiana might respond by saying that Indiana's geography did not provide the right kind of conditions for creating surfers. The same can be said about civilization: most of the regions of the world did not have a geography that was suitable for the creation of cities. Historians and archaeologists have developed a hazy definition of what a civilization consists of. For a city to receive the blue ribbon of "civilization," it must have contained a population of five to ten thousand inhabitants, been organized around a center, and contained a hierarchy, and some kind of record keeping/writing had to have been practiced by some of the city's inhabitants.

Generally speaking, the development of cities created new pressures on human societies, which required, in turn, new solutions. This process forced the development of human ingenuity, and so city life led to the development of record keeping, plumbing systems, architecture, and so forth.

This provides a nice logic to the concept of geographic determinism, which goes like this: Humans are equal, but the geography they settled on was not. The regions of the world that had the best geography were the regions where cities first formed, and those cities forced human beings to create new solutions to their new problems.

History does not produce neat logical equations, however. Cities did not always lead human beings to record keeping and writing. The Mayan,

INTRODUCTION

Incan, and Aztec societies of Latin America each produced cities without developing record keeping or a formal system of writing.

This leads to a more nuanced philosophy of history, one where historians might identify the kind of factors that might raise the probability that a certain outcome will occur. Cities should be viewed as greenhouses for ideas. In the same way that greenhouses create the right kind of conditions for plants to grow, cities create the right kind of conditions for ideas to grow. This does not always mean that ideas will grow, however, which leaves room for human agency to affect history.

With these principles in mind, the history of civilization might be thought of as occurring in four distinct phases.

## Phase I: The Dots Form

Think of the early civilizations of the world as "dots" formed in isolation from each other. Each civilization grew more or less separately as hunter-gatherer bands settled in various regions of the world. In the Middle East, the crop that allowed for the development of civilization was wheat; in India and China, it was rice. All civilizations were established next to sources of fresh running water.

## Phase II: The Dots in Eurasia Connect

Once the early "dots" of civilization formed, they were connected through a process of trade and conquest. The "greatest" connector of antiquity was Alexander the Great, who brought together the cultures of Persia, India, Egypt, and Greece. The long spears that Alexander's soldiers carried as they marched in a phalanx might be thought of as pencils.

The Romans later connected the dots of the various civilizations that would come to be known as the West. In the seventh century, the Muslims would connect the dots of Indian, Middle Eastern, and Eastern European civilizations, and then, in the thirteenth century, the Mongols would bring China into the full picture by conquering all of the major civilizations that could be found in the dry northern parts of Eurasia.

When the dots connected, this allowed for technology, ideas, and viruses to spread. Ideas and technologies would synthesize in new cultures. A new technology might have multiple uses, but as long as it stays only within one culture, it will likely be seen to have only one use. For example, the Chinese discovered the recipe for gunpowder but used it primarily for fireworks and rudimentary weapons. When gunpowder diffused westward after the Mongol armies connected China with the rest of the world, it combined with European church-bell technology and in time became the cannon.

Usually, after the dots of a society connected in Eurasia, a period of translation followed, which, in turn, led to a period of cultural, political, or technological advancement. Sometimes, however, a cultural feature in a region could hold this process back. The Romans, for example, used a cumbersome numeral system that prevented the creation of higher-level mathematics in the West for centuries. Sometimes cultures deliberately stopped the progress of technology and the spread of ideas because either or both might threaten the ruling structure. This occurred in the late fifteenth century when the Ottoman Empire banned the printing press.

## Phase III: The Bigger Picture Displaces the Smaller Picture

Given the thesis applied here, one might think that when Christopher Columbus found two continents' worth of "dots" in 1492, a new process of connection would occur between the Old and the New Worlds. Unfortunately, this did not happen. Instead, the picture created via the connections in Eurasia was picked up and transplanted in the Americas (and Australia, and New Zealand, and to some extent southern Africa).

The connect-the-dots process occurred much more easily from west to east because plants and people could move through similar climatic zones. Connecting dots that were situated from north to south proved to be much more difficult, and so the picture in the Americas never developed as fully as it had in Eurasia. The Eurasian explorers and conquistadors who arrived in the New World after 1492 possessed the guns, germs, and steel that the Eurasian picture had provided. This ensured that the picture of the Americas would not so much be connected as displaced.

## Phase IV: Globalization

Once the societies of Eurasia, and particularly Europe, were transplanted across the world, Western societies grew in strength so that it became

INTRODUCTION

possible for the West to dominate, but not displace, the civilizations of the East and create a new global picture. The dots of the world became connected into a globalized picture that is dominated by ethical and scientific philosophies that originated in Western Civilization. With the dots connected, the often bloody process of connection changes form, and the societies of the world become relatively peaceful and interconnected. But globalization certainly has its discontents.

# CHAPTER ONE
# HUMAN MIGRATIONS

## Dot 1: Humanity, Off and Running

Only two animals in nature are capable of running for long distances, and they are horses and humans. Both species share a feature that is rare in the animal kingdom: they can sweat. No animal can run for long distances without the ability to keep its internal system cool, and sweating is the most efficient cooling system found in nature.

The efficiency of sweating can be seen by comparing this cooling system to that of dogs. Dogs have to pant because this brings in air that cools their brains and bodies. The leftover condensation from this process can be found on a dog's nose, which is wet and cool.

Dogs have relatively inefficient cooling systems because their ancestors, wolves, evolved in cold climates where it was more important to have a good heating system (fur) than a cooling system. Humans, by contrast, evolved in the hot climate of Eastern Africa and continue to carry the legacy of that geography. Humans could only venture into the world's colder climates by killing animals and stealing their cold-weather adaptations in the form of furs and skins.

Two professors, one a biologist at the University of Utah named Dennis Bramble and the other a paleoanthropologist from Harvard named Daniel Lieberman, have developed a novel theory as to how the human ability to sweat, which allowed humans to run for long distances, might have made humans effective hunters.

CHAPTER ONE

Obviously, the ability to run at low or medium speeds for a long distance could not have been useful for evading predators capable of knocking down a human runner within just a few yards. However, while humans cannot run faster than animals such as cheetahs and antelope, we can run *longer*. This may have made it possible for human hunters to chase after prey animals until those animals simply overheated and sat down in exhaustion, which would have made them easy to kill. This hunting technique was observed among the Kalahari Bushmen in southern Africa, who would run antelope down in extremely hot weather and then kill them for meat.

## Dot 2: Cool Brains

Human beings consist of about 70 percent water, and water must be constantly taken into the body through eating or drinking, and then sent out of the body in the form of urine and sweat. Sweat especially helps to regulate the human body temperature. This is important because, as the Second Law of Thermodynamics states, "work creates heat." Large engines need efficient cooling machines.

The paleontologist John Wheeler has hypothesized that by standing upright on two legs, humans were able to reduce the amount of solar radiation they absorbed. This, in turn, allowed the human body to stop expending so much energy on the creation of body fur. Thick hair was really only needed on the area of the body that received the most sunlight, which was the head and the shoulders.

Humans therefore possessed a remarkable ability shed heat, and it can be said that the human cooling system is the most efficient in nature. This, according to Wheeler, allowed humans to evolve large brains in relation to the human body size. The brain takes in something like 16 percent of all the calories consumed; a large organ like that, which takes in energy and produces heat, could only evolve in a mammal that could keep it cool.

## Dot 3: Out of Africa Twice

Having looked at some of the interesting features of the human anatomy (and there are more besides), it's now possible to put modern humans into prehistorical context. The scientific name for modern humans is *Homo sapien sapien* (which means "wise, wise man"—you get titles like that when a species names itself), and both the DNA and archaeological evidence point to eastern Africa as the region where *Homo sapien sapien* and the immediate ancestor of that species, *Homo sapiens*, evolved.

First, it must be understood that *Homo sapiens* evolved in a world where several other human-like species were living simultaneously. In the same way that a cocker spaniel and a poodle can both trace their genetic ancestry to the wolf (even as all three exist at the same time), both *Homo sapiens* and Neandertals can trace their ancestry back to *Homo erectus*.

It should also be noted that a set of *Homo erectus* parents never gave birth to a *Homo sapien* child. Evolution works gradually, and in the same way that we can never call a person an adolescent on a single day but can point to a time period of that person's life that we would call adolescence, we cannot point to a single individual who might be called the first *Homo sapien*. Instead, there comes a time when a population might be referred to as a new species, and precisely when this actually began is open to argument and interpretation.

About 1.5 million years ago, a population of *Homo erectus* lived in Africa, and the group split into three. One group left and settled in Europe, where over time they evolved into the Neandertal people. One group stayed home in Africa and evolved into *Homo sapiens*. At some point between about ten and fifty thousand years ago, Africa's *Homo sapiens* developed the ability to speak. This likely occurred as a result of an adaptation of the voice box.

Jared Diamond calls this evolutionary shift the "Great Leap Forward," as the ability to speak caused changes in the neurological structure of the human brain. *Homo sapiens*, armed with speech and complex brains, then moved out of Africa and into Europe and Asia. There were almost certainly proto-humans, descendants of the original group of *Homo erectus* peoples, living in Asia at that time as well, so those early *Homo sapiens* who migrated out of Africa would have intermingled with other human-like species.

This, of course, raises lots of questions. Did humans and Neandertals mate, and if they did, could they produce offspring together? The answer, based on modern DNA evidence, is yes. Neandertal DNA can still be found in modern humans to varying degrees. The more obvious and disturbing question is: Where are the Neandertals?

# CHAPTER ONE

Humans might have outcompeted the Neandertals for resources, driving them into extinction, or it is possible that early humans simply killed them all off in a prehistoric bout of genocide. Given the lack of evidence, any hypothesis is mere speculation. There may very well have been several other human-like species in the prehistoric era that modern scientists do not know about.

In 2003, several small and human-like skeletons were discovered in Indonesia. After careful study, most scientists concluded that these skeletons represented a separate human species now extinct.

Sometime in prehistory, for whatever reason, *Homo sapien sapiens* survived while their evolutionary cousins did not. As the *Homo sapien sapien* species settled around the globe, slight variations in skin tone and eye shape evolved. Humanity was not separate long enough for deep evolution to occur, but superficial genetic changes led to the development of what might loosely be called "race."

Why human beings evolved different skin tones is a matter of debate, but there is likely a correlation between skin tone and the amount of sunlight that a geographic region receives. Genes get passed on in one of two ways: either the gene gives an organism an attribute that helps it to survive or the gene gives an organism an attribute that helps it to mate. Since the sun provides Vitamin D, it's possible that there is a correlation between geography and skin tone. The first *Homo sapien sapiens* would have had dark skin, but as humans migrated into regions with less sunlight, the environment might have favored people with lighter skin tones. Those who had less pigmentation could more easily absorb the weak or infrequent rays of sunlight found in northern regions like Scotland or Norway, where people frequently have fair skin and red or blond hair.

At first, this looks like a neat pattern. People in central Africa, where sunlight is abundant, have very dark pigmentation, while individuals in northern Africa have a dusky complexion, Mediterranean peoples have olive-colored skin, and northern European peoples have light skin. Eskimos, however, do not fit into the pattern, as they have fairly dark skin but live in a northern climate; they tend to get Vitamin D from their diet of seal meat and fat.

Geography and the whims of sexual selection probably explain why there are slight variations among the peoples of the world in other ways.

Why can men in some parts of the world grow thick beards while men in other parts of the world barely have any facial hair? Why do the peoples of Asia and parts of Southeast Asia have an epicanthic fold (slight slant to the eyes), while peoples of European descent have rounded eyes? It's probably the case that, for whatever reason, the people of those societies found those traits attractive, and so the genes got passed on and became dominant in the population.

## Dot 4: North American Animals Evolve Large Size

Early humans traveled in hunter-gatherer tribes; these tribes would be the primary social configuration of humanity for over one hundred thousand years. City life created the kinds of conditions that made the development of writing necessary, and since hunter-gatherers did not live in cities, they never developed writing. This means that we have few records detailing the existence of the people living in those tribes. Archaeological evidence does indicate, however, that these early humans lived in a terrifying world inhabited by woolly mammoths, saber-toothed tigers, and predatory birds that stood as tall as a single-story house.

Evolution often favors size; predatory animals have to be big enough to defend themselves against rivals for mates, and they also have to possess enough size to be able to take down their prey. Smaller predatory animals often compensate for a lack of size by hunting in packs. At the same time, prey animals evolve to be quick, stealthy, or big. This explains why the biggest animals, like mastodons and mammoths, were herbivores, and why North America was once populated by such exotic mammals as three-ton sloths and beavers the size of small cars.

However, it seems that when humans arrived, these enormous animals suddenly disappeared from North America.

## Dot 5: The Human Ability to Throw

The historian Alfred Crosby has given some insight into what might have driven the big animals of North America into extinction. He notes that one of the very distant ancestors of humans was an arboreal animal called an *australopithecine*. Because australopithecines lived in trees, they had to evolve a rotator cuff for swinging, an opposable thumb for gripping branches, and depth perception to avoid running into tree trunks.

It turns out that this is the exact same "equipment" necessary for throwing. The descendants of australopithecines left the trees but kept the rotator cuff, thumb, and sense of depth perception. *Homo erectus*, Neandertals, and *Homo sapiens* all possessed the right equipment for throwing, but *Homo sapiens* are the ones who managed to develop the ability into a deadly art form.

Humans are the only animals that can throw accurately and therefore kill or harm another animal from a safe distance. When humans migrated into North America, they would have encountered massive and mostly immobile animals that could not escape the spears and darts thrown by the nimble hominid aliens who had just arrived. A re-creation of a woolly mammoth might look horrifying to modern humans, but to our ancestors a mammoth probably looked like a giant steak.

The theory that human beings eradicated the big animals of North America by hunting the herbivores to extinction, and therefore depriving the large carnivores of their prey, is sometimes called the "Blitzkrieg" theory. The only wild animals in North America to survive were the small and quick ones that could escape from human hunters. Some animals, like the beaver, simply shrank over time as the biggest were singled out for hunting.

At some point, humans began to express an eerie form of ingenuity, one that broke them free from the bounds of the glacially slow process of biological evolution. Human beings started building themselves extra joints in the form of an atlatl. The atlatl looks simple—it's a just a jointed stick with a section that could hold a small, arrow-like dart—but it represents humanity's movement into cultural evolution.

Humans could whip objects like rocks and spears at animals, and presumably each other, because of the long, jointed arm. Why not make the arm longer by adding another joint? This simple process allowed human hunters to whip a dart with greater velocity, thus improving the killing capacity of the hunter. A process that once took millions of years, that of evolving an adaptation biologically, could now be done in a few minutes or hours. Now we can see that virtually every form of human ingenuity can be seen as a culturally evolved human trait (e.g., computers are extrapolations of human memory).

## Dot 6: Wheat and the Food Surplus

Civilization is inspired by city life, and it could not have grown if human beings had to keep moving, as they did while living in hunter-gatherer bands. No great works of architecture were ever produced by nomadic peoples because the necessity for buildings did not exist. The rise of civilization required that people stay in one place for an extended length of time, which meant the food supply had to stay in one place.

Sometime around ten thousand years ago, people in the Fertile Crescent region of the Middle East started planting wheat and barley. Wheat is a durable crop, with a short growing season, and the "stubble" that is left over after harvest can be used to feed livestock animals such as goats. Wheat is made up of carbohydrates, but if it is fed to animals, it spurs the development of animal muscle and milk, which are the main sources of protein and fat for humans.

Diamond has written that wheat, like most crops, travels well along a latitude line but not longitudinally. Climate and geography, as a general rule, are more uniform from east to west than from north to south, which helps to explain why wheat was able to advance in an east-to-west direction. Nothing of the sort could have happened, for example, in continents like South America or Africa, where the continents are situated along a north-south axis. Few, if any, plants can survive in both a North African desert and a Central African tropical forest.

## Dot 7: Animals and Disease Origins

In the fifteenth, sixteenth, and seventeenth centuries, diseases brought by Eurasian explorers (who happened to be European) nearly erased the native people who lived in the New World. It is estimated that around 90 percent of the native peoples living in North America, for example, died of smallpox and probably some combination of other diseases brought over from Eurasia.

The effects of these diseases represent the worst demographic crisis in all of history, and it presents the most disturbing question in world history: Were the Native Americans doomed from the moment that people living in the Fertile Crescent domesticated animals? Jared Diamond has made the case that all of the diseases that have killed humans through-

# CHAPTER ONE

out history, including the flu and smallpox, evolved in animals and were transmitted to humans.

In order to find where these diseases originate, one must simply find where the animals that carried them lived prior to domestication. Very few animals, it turns out, can be effectively domesticated. Only those that give birth regularly, eat foods that humans don't, and can behave themselves in captivity are useful as food animals. The same characteristics, plus size, are needed for animals that engage in farm work.

Cows, goats, pigs, horses, and sheep all could be found in North Africa, West Asia, and/or the Fertile Crescent region of the Middle East. The only animals that met the criteria for domestication in the Americas were the llama (found in South America), the dog, and the turkey (found in North America). The natives of these regions could not domesticate animals they did not have.

Once people in the Fertile Crescent domesticated animals, they settled in one place and often came into contact with animal dung as well as human sewage. In the absence of germ theory, this meant that diseases wrought havoc on human populations. This is where the brutal mathematics of evolution reshaped societies: by constantly weeding out those peoples with weak immune systems, the viruses and germs that came from animals created an environmental pressure that led to the evolution of powerful immunities in human survivors.

In Eurasia, for thousands of years, human immune systems and various diseases would engage in a savage evolutionary arms race, where only the humans with the strongest immune systems could survive long enough to make babies, and only the strongest viruses could break through the evolved immune systems.

Arms races occur in nature all the time, and the most dramatic example is the arms race that occurs between cheetahs and gazelles on the African savannah. Since only the quickest cheetahs can catch gazelles, and since only the quickest gazelles can escape cheetahs, both animals have evolved to be able to run at ridiculously fast speeds.

What would happen if someone transported the African cheetahs into a field full of sheep? The answer is obvious, and the same general principle can also be applied to what happens when a virus that has been locked in an arms race with certain immune systems is suddenly transplanted to a region where the human immune systems have not faced the same evolutionary pressures.

In the Americas, the big animals that the original human hunters had encountered soon died off, and animals of such immense size would not have been useful for domestication anyway, as it takes too long for them to mature in size. The mega-animals of the Americas lacked the kind of characteristics that would have made them useful to humans in ways beyond giving meat.

Beasts of burden, such as oxen, which can be used to plow fields, also gave another advantage to early humans who could domesticate them: they represented the first step of a technological evolution that would increasingly challenge human creativity. The ox and plow is the distant ancestor of the modern tractor, and it's fair to say that societies lacking the ox and plow would, therefore, also lack the tractor unless that technology was imported from elsewhere.

## Connecting the Dots

Humans and Neandertals both evolved from a common ancestor called *Homo erectus*, which originated in central and eastern Africa. When one group of *Homo erectus* migrated into Europe, they evolved over time into the Neandertal species. One group of *Homo erectus*, which had stayed in Africa, evolved over time into the modern *Homo sapien sapien* species, or modern humans.

As humans settled around the globe, they had a tendency to displace the other human-like species they encountered. This likely happened in Asia and in Europe, although exactly what eradicated the Neandertal species is not clear. Humans continued to settle the globe and evolved very slight variations in their phenotype depending upon the pressures of both natural and sexual selection. The relatively rapid rise of *Homo sapien sapiens* to a position of dominance over their fellow hominids meant that soon humans were able to settle across the globe.

Geography granted certain randomly assigned advantages to early humans who settled around the globe. Wheat and domesticated animals turned out to be the factors that would begin the process of creating inequality between the societies of Eurasia and the societies of the New

CHAPTER ONE

World and the various isolated regions of Earth. The implications of these advantages would not be fully observed until European explorers left Eurasia, but their guns (the development of which will be detailed later), germs, and steel proved to be the decisive factors in moving the Eurasian picture to the New World. The Eurasian picture would eventually displace the previously connected American picture even while integrating the Native American plague survivors into a new globalized picture of trade.

The scientific processes that drove this process would not be understood until centuries after the conquest and subjugation of the New World and various isolated regions of the planet had occurred. This means that early explorers and settlers from Europe brought not only their diseases with them during their travels but also their beliefs about disease. Europeans tended to see diseases as the wrath of God, a belief that would have larger implications.

## CHAPTER TWO
# THE DOTS FORM

### Dot 1: Sumer

Sumer, in modern-day Iraq, sprouted next to the Tigris and Euphrates rivers. The development of an urban center caused the creation of a rudimentary economy based upon the development of specialized jobs. Productive agriculture meant that some people could do work other than looking for nourishment. Those specialized workers would then trade their skills for other people's goods. When such interactions took place between just a few individuals, keeping track of money owed and paid proved to be easy. However, as the network of trade interactions grew more complex, some method of recording those interactions proved necessary.

The first mathematicians used what looked like large clay Hershey's Kisses to keep track of their interactions. This allowed for addition and subtraction. After some intermediary changes, accountants realized they could just make a mark on a clay tablet and keep track of the interactions in this way.

We could think of this as the outsourcing of memory to a clay tablet. Human memory, having evolved on the African savannah, did not have the necessary equipment to keep track of a series of sometimes complicated economic arrangements, so humans gave the job to the tablet. (This process continues, almost *ad infinitum*, today with computers.)

Of course, it is no great leap to see that when one can record numeric transactions in such a way, it is also possible to symbolize words. The Sumerians used the latter concept to record what surely had been a long-standing myth, that of Gilgamesh, about a hero who wanders the world in grief after a devastating flood. This is fitting—the rivers that gave life to civilization also formed the central concept of humanity's first work of literature. Religious towers, called ziggurats, attracted worshipers and gave off an aura of power.

The religious impulse to build sky-scraping buildings, be they pyramids, minarets, or the gothic cathedrals of medieval Europe, is almost catholic among early societies. In the modern world, where the dollar functions as a kind of god and banks act as its cathedral, one can see the same impulse in the multi-storied buildings dedicated to commerce in the world's major cities.

Eventually, the Sumerians fell to the Akkadians and their imperious leader, Sargon. The Akkadians then lost to the Babylonians. One of the Babylonian kings, Hammurabi, united Mesopotamia between 1750 and 1800 BCE, and he had a law code commissioned and named after him. This code, featuring its crude "eye for an eye" style of punishments, represents one of humanity's earliest attempts to codify the law rather than leaving it to the whims of the powerful.

## Dot 2: Egypt

Historians divide the lengthy history of Egypt up into multiple periods, many defined by changes in the archaeological record. Summarizing such vast knowledge would take this narrative on too long of a detour. However, the Egyptians created many important inventions and concepts that would, in time, benefit civilizations beyond their borders, and so the focus here is on those contributions.

In Egypt, the digging of irrigation canals off of the Nile facilitated the creation of a rudimentary geometry, necessary for measuring the square-like plots of land. Those plots of land could then be taxed, thus giving wealth and power to a growing centralized state. The Egyptians worshiped a pantheon of mostly nature gods, probably because the Egyptians themselves were under such tremendous pressure to control the uncontrollable weather patterns. The pharaoh himself came to be seen as a god (the old emperor-is-a-god political philosophy would have a good run in societies around the world throughout history, up until recently), and the development of pyramids to serve the imperial ego required standard forms of measurement.

And then there was the mother Nile herself, unruly and temperamental, but not ultimately unpredictable. At some point, a bright Egyptian stargazer looked up at the considerable night sky (something to behold in desert regions before the polluting light of electricity) and noticed that the random pinpricks of light actually formed patterns. Even better, those patterns moved. If one could be sure and stare at the same patch of sky every night, then it became possible to discern the regular appearance and disappearance of certain constellations and bright spots. From there, one could connect a certain pattern in the sky with the annual flooding of the Nile.

Soon enough the Egyptians, like many other ancient societies, discerned that the sky can be considered a celestial, and reliable, calendar. The Egyptians also developed a pictographic language, although its connections with commerce are not as clear as in Sumer.

## Dot 3: India

Historians of early India tend to grit their teeth in frustration over the lack of sources. Not much is known about the early Indus River valley settlements, other than the fact that the inhabitants developed a sophisticated plumbing system. They did not develop writing. At some point, a settlement of dark-skinned people in the south, known as the Dravidians, was overrun by chariot-riding conquerors from modern-day Iran. These warriors, referred to as Aryans (most people associate this term with Nazi Germany because in Hitler's cockamamie racial historiography, he traced the origins of the German master race to these relatively light-skinned Middle Eastern warmongers), carried with them many of the traits associated with India up to the present day. In fact, "Aryan" is a linguistic term, referring to those who spoke the language.

Most notably, the Aryans brought Hinduism, Sanskrit, and the caste system. "Caste" translates to "color" and potentially has a dual meaning. Perched atop this new system were the light-skinned Aryans, while the mostly dark-skinned Dravidians got placed at the bottom. However, the truer meaning of "caste" is that different positions on the scale corresponded with a color. At the top were the Brahmins, or the priestly caste,

CHAPTER TWO

and at the bottom the Untouchables, sometimes referred to as the Children of God. One could not move up or down the system in this life; they instead had to hope to be reincarnated upward over time, thus calcifying the social layers.

India, a massive subcontinent spanning three different climatic zones, never achieved much in the way of unity even after the Aryan invasion. Political fragmentation, religious separation, and a massive population were to become India's trademarks.

## Dot 4: China and the Shang

In China, the experiment of civilization occurred in a petri dish separate from those in the Middle East, and rice, not wheat, provided the main source of calories infusing the growth of large-scale settlements. The "dots" of the early river valley settlements seem to have been connected via conquest by a set of chariot-riding conquerors who established a dynasty of sorts, known now as the Shang, by about 1500 BCE.

Everything that historians know about the Shang is based upon archaeological evidence. Life in Shang China probably did not differ dramatically from the original river valley civilizations, although it does appear that some of the more macabre aspects of the early settlements (such as the old staple of human sacrifice) slowed or stopped during Shang rule. The Chinese had developed a symbolic language by this time, with characters scratched onto bones.

Nonetheless, the Shang established monumental palaces and lavish tombs for the dead important people. This tendency to waste massive sums of labor and money as a means of keeping the rain off the royal dead must have had some further social purpose, perhaps showing the worth of living royal family members, for it to have been so prevalent in every culture.

## Dot 5: The Zhou

At some time in roughly 1000 BCE, the Zhou Dynasty took control of China's politics. To justify a sudden takeover of power, the Zhou configured the "Mandate of Heaven" concept. A beautiful piece of circular reasoning, the philosophy of the mandate proved both simple and durable. It simply stated that those who deserved to rule China would do so. If the emperor lost the throne, due to droughts, rebellion, or conquest, that was a sign from Heaven that the mandate had been revoked.

The Zhou endured for an impressive seven centuries, but they never had much of a central core. China remained governed mostly by local warlords who used overpowering armies to keep the peasants in line. The relatively chaotic rule of the Zhou led at least one political thinker, called Confucius in the West, to stress the importance of order in society.

## Dot 6: Confucius

The life of Confucius (551–478 BCE) fits comfortably into the middle of the Zhou era. Though he never personally exercised political power, Confucius's philosophy came to guide China for several centuries. He occupied himself as a political adviser, and, like Socrates, he never wrote a word that survived. Also like Socrates, Confucius's students later recorded his best insights.

Before stating what Confucianism is, it may be best to note what it is not, which is religious or scientific. Confucius showed no interest in the afterlife, and faith as defined by the big three monotheistic religions (Judaism, Christianity, and Islam) factored not at all into Confucian ideology. Confucius's intellect seems to have never been piqued or troubled by scientific questions, such as the fundamental essence of matter, either.

Confucianism functioned as a purely political philosophy focusing on the necessity of order. Chaos ensued when people did not know their societal places. A Confucian sense of order could be superimposed on the family, the country, and even the world. In short, the father should be the head of the household, the emperor the head of China, and China the leader of the planet. Respect for the father went by the title of "filial piety," and all problems in a Chinese household could be traced to a lack of such piety.

China lacked many of the individualistic concepts of the West, as the expectations were that young people would marry a spouse who had been selected by their parents. Teenage rebellion, for example, was never romanticized, as it would be occasionally in the European arts. In China such romantic rebellions would have invited revulsion. Had the Chinese ever staged a version of *Romeo and Juliet*, it would have been short, as Juliet's father would have quickly ended the whole thing.

CHAPTER TWO

When people tried to move out of their proper stations, discord followed, and to Confucius such a thing was unacceptable.

## Dot 7: The Chinese Alphabet

Archaeologists have found evidence of early Chinese characters painted onto bones since the Shang Dynasty. Over time, the Chinese alphabet expanded into thousands of characters. In practice, this made mass production of books difficult. Scholars in this era before the printing press copied books by hand. Or, as in the case of the Chinese schools, they tended to set up the text on raised stone where copies could be made by pressing ink over the paper (think of a grave rubbing).

Such a setup made it nearly impossible to publish and promulgate new ideas, as old books and concepts were set down in stone. This would not matter for centuries, as the rest of the world remained rather far behind China's culture. However, once the printing press evolved in Western Europe (the basic idea being derived from China long before Gutenberg in fifteenth-century Germany), the comparison between a phonetic alphabet and an ideographic one made all the difference in the modern world. An ideographic script is almost as cumbersome on a printing press as it is on a computer keyboard—hardly a good fit for the rapid creation and spread of ideas.

Can China's legendary cultural conservatism be linked to its alphabet? Can the modern world's dynamism be linked to a phonetic script, which allows for the rapid creation of new material via typing on a computer? The existence of such questions shows that the ancient world still endures even today.

## Dot 8: Daoism

The founder of Daoism, Laozi, may or may not have existed. If he did, then he would have taught around the year 500 BCE and his life would have overlapped with that of Confucius. To restate an earlier point, Asian religions did not put emphasis on faith in the way that the monotheistic religions did. Instead, Asian religions encouraged practitioners to attain a state of mind or state of being.

Religion was seen as a practice rather than a set of beliefs. One could be, under this concept, a Confucian who practiced Daoism without encountering any religious conflict. No wars of religion, in the vein of "my belief is better than yours," mar the pages of Chinese history, as the Asian concept of religion did not lend itself to such battles.

The writings, mostly aphorisms, associated with Laozi appear to be intended to confuse the reader. The notion, perhaps, was to force the Daoist practitioner into a state of contemplation. Then, while one was sitting on a rock trying to untangle the meaning in the master's words, one's mind was pulled away from the mundane concerns of the world. Thus, without intending to, one has reached a peaceful state of mind. The Daoist practitioner travels a course of paradox, trying to reach a destination that one can only reach when one stops trying to find it. (Now, go sit under a tree and ponder that last sentence for a while.)

## Dot 9: Zhou Collapse and the Warring States

Between 402 and 221 BCE China's political core deteriorated. Power dissolved from the center to a variety of warlords, each governing a comparatively small patch of territory. Governmental collapses happen frequently throughout history. When central governments collapse, power reverts to local warlords, who typically hold society together through the use of violence.

Those with wealth or land had to build up defenses—castles, in many cases—against marauding rival armies. Wealthy landholders hired mercenaries for protection. The peasants often worked the land in exchange for a measure of security against a highly unstable outside world.

In China, for about two hundred years the warlords held sway, and none controlled enough soldiers or harnessed enough power to conquer the others. That is, not until 221, when Qin Shi Huangdi became emperor.

## Dot 10: Qin Shi Huangdi

One of the localized warlords from the Zhou era emerged as a true political strongman. Qin Shi Huangdi controlled the Qin Dyansty and, over time, conquered his rival groups. His power snowballed until he controlled a massive section of territory and eventually overthrew the last of the Zhou emperors.

Qin Shi Huangdi despised the aristocracy, seeing them as the main cause of China's political fragmentation, and brutally established central rule. Naturally, he took a liking to the philosophy of legalism, which proscribed brutal punishments (such as drawing and quartering or burning at the stake) for minor infractions. Such bloodshed was given moral cover by aphorisms such as "water appears gentle but men often drown, whereas fire appears harsh and men are seldom burnt." Very poetic, one supposes, unless you are the one with your appendages tied to rampaging horses.

But China did centralize, preventing it from becoming a Far Eastern version of India. The language was codified and made official while forms of weights and measures became standardized across the dynasty's realms. Qin Shi Huangdi commissioned a Great Wall to mark the borders of his empire and employed typically brutal methods to conscript workers into the cause.

Then he started drinking mercury and spent his time hunting for a magical fish.

As time went on, Qin Shi Huangdi obsessed over immortality. It was as if, having conquered the known world, he could only focus on the fact that death would take it from him. Mercury, an odd substance that looks solid but acts like a liquid, was rumored to have medicinal qualities when ingested. Of course, it likely poisoned the emperor's mind. As for the fish, well, Chinese storytellers had been spreading the tale of linguistically gifted fish for centuries, and Qin Shi Huangdi thought that if he could grab hold of this talking fish, he would be granted eternal life. It probably sounded like a good idea at the time.

Eventually, unconvinced that he could live forever, Qin Shi Huangdi made plans to conquer the afterlife. He demanded an army be created out of terra cotta for his tomb. These warriors would accompany him into the spirit world. Whether they did is not known.

## Connecting the Dots

After the human species spread across the planet, certain geographic regions proved better for the development of civilizations than others. River valleys provided the basic necessities of running water and generally fertile soil. The commonality among the earliest civilizations can be found in their locations along bodies of fresh water. Cities tended to grow organically from these water structures, and these settlements produced new needs that required new forms of inventive thought, which in turn spiraled off into other innovative concepts.

Historians generally define a civilization as being a settlement with a significant population, urban center, some political structure, and record keeping (numbers and/or letters). Although archaeologists have uncovered large-scale settlements at Çatal Höyük in Turkey and Jericho in the Middle East, neither of these sites provides evidence of record keeping; therefore, Sumer is the first place to have the blue ribbon of "civilization" pinned to its metaphorical chest.

Sumer, Egypt, and India each grew up around river valleys and developed, to a certain degree, high levels of technological complexity. Indian history, while remaining nebulous, nonetheless developed similarities to Egypt in particular. In the same way that the Aryans conquered the Dravidians with chariots, the Egyptians periodically faced challenges from chariot-riding Hittites to the south. Inhabitants of all three regions worshiped a variety of deities, mostly nature gods.

Perhaps the most sophisticated religious philosophy came from the Hindus. The Upanishads (meaning "to sit next to," as in to sit next to a great teacher) and the Vedas certainly had been transferred to the religious followers for centuries in oral form before being written down in Sanskrit. The notion central to Hinduism was that one could rise to a state of being called *Nirvana*. Asian religions put little emphasis on faith as it was later understood by the monotheists; rather, these religions tended to encourage followers to search for a state of mind.

## CHAPTER THREE
# GREECE

### Dot 1: Geography

*Greece* is an umbrella term used to describe the often disparate nation-states, many of them islands, that existed in the Aegean Sea and on the Peloponnesian peninsula. Each of these islands represented different political systems. Indeed, one could find examples of virtually all political configurations among the islands, including oligarchy, monarchy, and democracy. The Greek geography led to the same type of disunity and political fragmentation that existed in India. The difference between Greece and India, however, was in size.

India, as a subcontinent, straddles three climatic zones. Modern scientists count two thousand different ethnic groups in India, and in the modern era the money has to be printed in fifteen separate languages. The Greeks, by contrast, typically spoke the same language, shared an ethnic background, and existed in a much smaller geographic range that was knitted together by well-trodden sea paths.

Unlike the Indians, they did have the capacity to unify, when absolutely necessary, against a clear and present danger. The two major states of Greece, the fabled Sparta and Athens, represented two very different political philosophies but nonetheless understood each other well enough to form and break alliances.

CHAPTER THREE

## Dot 2: The *Iliad*

Classicists have been debating the origins and historical value of the *Iliad* and its companion, the *Odyssey*, for as long as the books have been studied. These epics detail events that supposedly occurred four or five centuries before they were recorded. The events are said to date from the twelfth century BCE, but writing did not come to Greece until the eighth century BCE. Legend has it that a blind poet named Homer composed the great works, but most classical scholars believe that the composition of the poems took place over a long period of time and bear the pen marks of many authors.

The scope of these epic poems is far too large to be summarized adequately here, but what the *Iliad* does *not* include is of interest. The *Iliad* concerns a single year of the Trojan War, but it contains no scene involving the Trojan Horse, nor does the book portray the invasion of Troy, even though both events are sometimes associated with the narrative.

Greek warriors fought for two reasons—one was to attain an honorable reputation. Most Greek men obsessed over what other people said about them. The Greeks would have been baffled by a character like Bruce Wayne/Batman or Clark Kent/Superman, as the idea of someone who has a secret identity and lets a masked alter ego gain all of the fame would have been nonexistent in their world. The desire for a great military reputation is what drives the book's main character, Achilles.

The *Iliad* begins with a Greek alliance outside the gates of Troy, in modern-day Turkey. One of the Trojan princes, Paris, had become obsessed with the wife of a Spartan king named Menelaus and kidnapped her (or she left voluntarily, or because of a complex set of interactions with the gods—the story varies). This led to a mass invasion by the Greek armies to avenge Menelaus's humiliation.

The war might have ended quickly, but Achilles, a god-like figure, refused to fight due to his hatred for King Agamemnon, Menelaus's brother and leader of the Greek forces. In a previous battle, Achilles had taken as a concubine the gorgeous wife, named Briseis, of one of his vanquished enemies. Agamemnon, consumed by lust, took her from Achilles, and as a result Achilles refused to take part in the battles.

Paris, protected by his father Priam and his warrior brother Hektor, at first retreats in battle from the Spartan husband whom he wronged.

Eventually, Hektor shames Paris into taking on Menelaus, and the Spartan king trounces his nemesis in one-on-one battle. The goddess Aphrodite rescues Paris before he can be killed and brings him back behind the walls of the city. Later Agamemnon, persuaded by a fellow warrior-king named Odysseus, decides in desperation to give Briseis back to Achilles, plus several other concubines, a small fortune, and access to the best spoils once Troy falls.

Achilles despises Agamemnon and says no. However, he does encourage his companion, the sensitive Patroclus, to join the fight. With the encouragement of his friend, Patroclus covers himself in the armor of Achilles, including a helmet that hides his face. The Greeks, thinking that Achilles has returned, take inspiration to fight heroically.

Patroclus, dressed as Achilles, throws himself at the Trojans with such ferocity that even the god Apollo, protector of the city, seems taken aback. Patroclus smashes in the head of Hektor's chariot driver, an act that causes Hektor to ride out and meet Patroclus-as-Achilles in battle. Hektor slays Patroclus and takes his enemy's armor.

Upon hearing about the death of his friend, Achilles falls into a black sorrow so deep he can do nothing but rub sand in his face and eyes. His wrath piqued, he will now fight. Plunging into the war, Achilles seeks out and eviscerates the younger brother of Hektor, leaving the young man clutching his newly liberated intestines. Hektor comes to fight, but Achilles cannot kill the man, as the gods turn Hektor to smoke time and again. The wrath of Achilles spills out onto the Trojan armies, which he punishes with god-like ferocity.

Again, Hektor comes out from behind the walls even though he knows he cannot win this fight. The poem details Achilles chasing Hektor around the walls of Troy four times before the gods convince Hektor to fight. It turns out to be bad advice, as Hektor is no match for the ultimate warrior. As Hektor falls dead, Achilles watches as his enemy's soul descends to Hades. Achilles then hooks the man's corpse up to a chariot and drags the body around the walls of the city.

Still consumed by grief, Achilles burns the corpse of Patroclus and then drags Hektor's body some more, until even the gods become disturbed by such psychopathic behavior. This bloody epic ends not with the destruction of Hektor, but with Hektor's father, Priam, coming out from the walls and throwing himself at Achilles's feet. He begs Achilles to stop dishonoring his son's body, and soon enough Achilles, choked up by memories of his own father and Patroclus, starts crying right along with the old man.

The *Iliad* ends with Achilles giving Priam back the mangled corpse of his son. "They all lived happily ever after" it is not.

## Dot 3: The *Odyssey*

Odysseus, a minor character in the *Iliad* (he's the one who persuaded Agamemnon to apologize to Achilles), is the main character of the *Odyssey*, which chronicles his attempts to get home after the ultimately successful ten-year siege of Troy. Odysseus had been the king of Ithaca in Greece when the Spartans summoned him to join their alliance after Helen was stolen by the Trojan Paris. (Please note that the following summation of the *Odyssey* is not presented in alignment with the actual structure of the work. Instead, the intent here is to present the major plot points in a linear narrative.)

When he left to join the fighting, Odysseus instructed his wife, Penelope, to marry again if he was not home by the time their baby son, Telemachus, had grown into a man.

In this story, Odysseus recounts the end of the war in Troy, and how he and his men tried to sail homeward to Ithaca. Odysseus reveals that Troy fell when the Greeks presented the Trojans with a gift of a massive wooden horse. Greek soldiers hid inside, and when the Trojans slept, the Greeks slipped out and destroyed the city. Paris, who had caused the whole mess to begin with, shot an arrow that felled Achilles, who had known he was fated to die.

Many adventures, including encounters with the gods and fantastical islands, keep the story moving at a rapid pace. Homer juxtaposes the main narrative of Odysseus and his men with Penelope's travails. Being both beautiful and the queen of Ithaca, Penelope attracted a lot of potential second husbands, known as the suitors. The suitors surrounded Penelope, trying to convince her that it was time to stop believing that Odysseus would return and to select a new husband and king.

This brilliant device increases the dramatic tension of Odysseus's adventures, as the audience can see that if Odysseus is too long delayed, Telemachus will grow to manhood, releasing Penelope from her marriage vows and forcing her to take a new husband. Homer depicts Penelope as a noble wife, as she never wavers in waiting for the return of Odysseus and never seems to feel anything but repulsed by the suitors.

Early on, Odysseus and his men find themselves on an island populated by several giant Cyclopes. Odysseus and his men become trapped in the cave of one Cyclops, and the giant is the only one powerful enough to move the boulder blocking the front of the cave. Odysseus attacks the monster, blinds his one eye, and then tells him that his name is Noe Body. When the Cyclops shrieks for help, he yells, "Noe Body is hurting me," which causes his fellow giants to turn around and go back home.

Clever as this escape is, it ultimately brings down the wrath of the sea god Poseidon. The blinded Cyclops turns out to be his son, and Poseidon's hunger for revenge drives him to sabotage the voyage of Odysseus. Meanwhile, Telemachus continues to grow, and the suitors continue to pressure Penelope to marry again.

Athena, Odysseus's divine ally, helps him to survive his journey and return home to Ithaca just in time to thwart a plot to kill Telemachus. Disguised as a beggar, Odysseus saves his son and then, still in disguise, wins an archery tournament staged by Penelope for the purpose of determining who her new husband would be. (Yes, this plot device will later show up in the Robin Hood tale.)

Odysseus wins but is twenty years older than when he'd left Ithaca, and Penelope can't tell whether the battle-scarred man in front of her is the same one who left her two decades before. She tests him for secret knowledge only the two of them would know, and when Odysseus passes, she finally embraces him. Odysseus has made it home.

## Dot 4: The Olympics, 776 BCE

There is something very revealing in the fact that the Greeks began their calendar with the year of the first Olympics in 776 BCE. The games serve as a microcosm of the Greek life. The Olympics provided a chance for Greek athletes to publicly compete, show off their bodies, and engage in individual accomplishment. No team sports ever got played in the Greek Olympics.

Greek society obsessed over the male body, and some scholars have noted the similarities between Greek culture, saturated as it was with images

CHAPTER THREE

(statues at least) of well-toned physiques, and the modern entertainment culture that revolves around impressive bodies. For the Greek man, reputation meant everything, and the Greeks were above all else public people. Men exercised and competed in the nude and prized the ability to orate and debate in public arenas. The Olympics displayed the Greek character.

## Dot 5: Sparta

Sometime around 630 BCE, the Spartans defeated a group of early Greeks called the Messenians and established a kingdom on the southern end of the Peloponnese. Once the Messenians became slaves, the Spartans used their freedom from manual labor to harden themselves into a master class of warriors. The Spartan governmental system possessed a rudimentary form of checks and balances, featuring two kings. The notion was that if the two kings squabbled with one another, then neither could grow too powerful. Sparta was not truly governed by the kings, however, but by a warrior code that has fascinated historians ever since.

Plutarch, the great biographer and historian of the ancient world, was so intrigued by the Spartans that he dedicated an entire book to their existence. He wrote a few hundred years after the Spartan state had ceased to exist, so much of he wrote may be legendary, but it is the legend of Sparta that people remember.

In Spartan society military strength was paramount, and the Spartan commanders believed that military strength was built upon individual character and toughness. Children belonged not to their parents but to the state. Male babies born with any defect threatened a society so dependent upon martial and mental toughness, and therefore were placed out in an open spot and left to die.

When a young man reached age seven, a council of elders placed boys into tribes and encouraged them to fight, steal, and hunt for survival. One legendary account of a boy caught stealing an animal tells of the child holding the beast under his shirt while being interrogated. When the boy died and his comrades discovered that the animal had dug out his guts during the questioning process, his toughness garnered praise.

When old enough, all men fought in the military. The Spartans developed the phalanx, a deep square of men each holding spear and shield. From a high vantage point, the phalanx must have looked a spiked turtle, but a deadly one. The Spartans trained the fear out their soldiers and cloaked themselves in a myth of invincibility. They would, in time, win the most legendary of ancient battles and become associated with a single place: Thermopylae.

## Dot 6: Athens

The Athenians began as a kingdom, and early Greek historians trace a royal line that lasted 450 years, but the historical veracity of the list appears as dubious as the events recorded in the *Iliad*. Eventually, the Athenians tossed away both the notion of a king and the title, adopting instead a political configuration featuring a chief justice, a commander-in-chief of the military, and a head priest. The leading figure was the chief justice, and over time the Athenians limited his term of office to a single year.

In 632 BCE a revolt led by an Olympic athlete named Cylon shattered the Athenian faith in their political system. Prior to this, both Athenian and Spartan law existed only in spoken form. The Athenians decided to encode their law in writing and gave the job to a lawyer named Draco.

Draco, not being particularly imaginative, prescribed death for just about everything. Murder someone? Death. Steal an apple? Death. And so forth. Draco's name lives on in the phrase "draconian," which indicates a particularly harsh code. Hardly anyone liked the laws, and it took just a few decades for another well-known lawgiver, Solon, to create a code with a greater level of fairness.

Solon, a good-time boy from a rich family, behaved like Robin Hood, forgiving the debts of the poor and divvying up the land in a more egalitarian fashion. The aristocracy and the money lenders, none too happy with any of his changes, dismantled this legal system shortly after the death of Solon. Democracy, of a kind, eventually came to Athens, but this society would never embrace equality.

Women had no vote, and slaves provided the labor for the fields. This was an era of built-in social stratification, and one must remember that the great epics of the era, the *Iliad* and the *Odyssey*, feature a plot surrounding Helen, a woman kidnapped into sexual slavery by Paris of the Trojans.

Unequal as it was, Greek society soon faced greater problems than legal squabbles and internal disputes over trade and culture: in the east the Persian threat grew.

CHAPTER THREE

## Dot 7: Persia

Cyrus the Great of Persia is the first known character in the ancient world to have the old "prophecy about the baby" narrative attached to his name. According to this legend, Cyrus's grandfather, a king of the Medes named Astyages, dreamed that Cyrus would grow up to overthrow him. (Herotodus detailed the rather gory details of this allegoric dream in his graphic classic *The Histories*.) Asytages dispatched a soldier, Harpagus, to kill his grandson, but the man could not bear to harm an infant and instead hid the child with a shepherd's family. The soldier presented another baby, recently dead of natural causes, to the king in the place of Cyrus.

Astyages found out about this deception and, in a nice touch, punished Harpagus by cooking the man's own son and secretly feeding the boy to him. In ancient narratives, prophecies act as spider webs; the harder one works to disentangle oneself from the inevitability of the future, the more tightly one comes to be bound. As it turns out, tricking a man into eating his cooked son is not the best way to earn loyalty. Harpagus subsequently conspired with Cyrus, who had grown up in the shepherd's care.

When Astyages sent Harpagus out to conquer and kill the now-grown Cyrus for the second time, Harpagus defected. Cyrus conquered his grandfather, just as the dream foretold, and subsequently let the man die quietly of old age. Cyrus, now king of the Medes and the Persians, then turned to defeat his great uncle Croesus of the Lydians (family reunions must have been awkward). This narrative, of a newborn baby who threatened the power of an evil leader, features prominently in ancient literature. In fact, it remains popular in our own time and has been recycled in both the *Star Wars* and *Harry Potter* epics.

Having conquered his family, the Greek general and historian Xenophon records that Cyrus established the first police state, where the government encouraged subjects to snitch on one another for any activity that might be perceived as revolutionary.

Babylon beckoned Cyrus (the conquering instinct is rarely satisfied), and he sent his armies to take the city, which they promptly realized they could not conquer. Instead, the soldiers forced a siege—a costly and time-consuming measure, as the invading army had to just sort of wait around outside until the people on the inside finished eating everything in the city and began starving.

But this was Cyrus, who was no fool, and the Tigris River ran through the middle of the city. Cyrus ordered his troops to dig canals away from the river, causing the water level to drop to nothing. The soldiers then plopped along in the muddy bed and went under the wall; afterward, they simply blended in with a group of partygoers in the street. They then opened the gates and on October 14, 539 BCE, the city fell.

The Jews, recently conquered by the Babylonians under Nebuchadnezzar, remember Cyrus fondly, as he gave them back their temple and returned some of their plundered religious artifacts. The Greeks took less satisfaction in the reign of Cyrus, as they now had to contend with a powerful empire, called the Achaemenid, to the east. Cyrus's descendants, it would turn out, retained the great man's thirst for conquest.

## Connecting the Dots

Ancient China and Greece deserve to be set aside from the other early civilizations because of the high level of intellectual sophistication attained by certain individuals in each, and because of the differing types of alphabets in each region. From the modern vantage point, we can see that each society complemented the other, developing forms of thought that their counterpart lacked.

While the Greeks engaged in philosophy as a kind of scientific inquiry but lacked any type of political unity, the Chinese went in the other direction, focusing on practical types of legal and social philosophy while largely ignoring the kind of scientific questioning that transfixed Greek thinkers. Likewise, the Greeks would obtain an alphabet from the Phoenicians (*phonetic*—get it?), a maritime power at the time. The Chinese opted for a pictographic language, where pictures stood for words rather than interchangeable sounds. This small difference in the layout of Western and Eastern languages would, over time, leave as deep an imprint on history as any other factor.

By the time of Cyrus, the fractured Greek city-states had formed into politically distinct entities, with the two most powerful being Sparta and Greece. The Greeks possessed a form of democracy, according to which landed males could vote in a public space. Eventually, citizenship became hereditary, so that a man would not lose his democratic voice even upon losing his land. The Spartans, however, assigned little honor to one's abil-

## CHAPTER THREE

ity to advocate for ideas. While Spartan government did feature some level of democracy for individuals over thirty years of age, no emphasis was given to debate.

Soon enough, the Persian shadow fell over the Greek borderlands to the east. The Athenians, historically leery of potential tyrants, took a vote and ostracized a power-hungry politician named Hippias. Hippias duly ran to the Persians, seeking their help in his scheme for revenge. The Persians sent the Athenians a letter demanding that the exiled tyrant-in-waiting be reaccepted into society or else. At about this time, the Greeks under Persian control rebelled. The first rumblings of an epic war could be heard.

## CHAPTER FOUR
# THE WARS

**Dot 1: The Sources**

Historians of the Persian Wars must make do with only the Greek side of the story, as we have no detailed version of the events from the Persian point of view. A man named Herodotus wrote the first work of history, which is titled, appropriately enough, *The Histories*. The title comes from the Greek word *historia*, meaning "inquiry." And inquire he did, walking around and asking questions about the past.

The next great historian, the one who chronicled the battles and political machinations between Sparta, Athens, and the many Greek city-states that became swept up in the Aegean maelstrom, went by the name of Thucydides. His book bears the marks of historical reliability. Herodotus seemed to revel in the sex and gore of the ancient world, while Thucydides took a more sober (and perhaps boring) approach.

The battles of the Peloponnesian War do not feature any legendary heroics, as did the Persian Wars, and to detail them here would represent too long a detour for this narrative. The focus, instead, will be on the causes and consequences.

The Persian Wars constitute only a small portion of Herodotus's accounts, but they have drawn the most attention because of the themes presented. Those themes—of free Greeks, outnumbered, battling against a massive Persian army dedicated to enslaving them—make up much of the historical character of the West. How much of what Herodotus wrote is true and how much is myth will never be known, and he's called both the "father of history" and the "father of lies." Either way, this is the story he told: After the death of Cyrus, a series of tedious and mysterious political plots unfolded in Persia. By 521 BCE, the new Persian king was named Darius, who may or may not have been the son of Cyrus. Almost always, in the case of empires, when confusion reigns after the death of a monarch or tyrant, the regions under domination take advantage of the situation by rebelling. Once he'd attained power, Darius faced a series of revolts by Greek city-states. The new Persian king remodeled the Persian army, training a loyal force and doing away with the typical mercenary force that most emperors made use of.

## Dot 2: Marathon

The Greek cities engaging in rebellion stole three hundred Persian ships and then entered the city of Sardis, setting it aflame. Darius responded by sending a fleet of warships to the city. The Persians tunneled under the city walls, an effective siege technique that collapsed the stone, and then enslaved the Greek population.

Unfortunately for Darius, the Greek weather made an enemy of him, and a freak storm crunched most of his ships against the jutting rocks that surrounded many of the Greek islands. Darius rebuilt and had another go at it a couple of years later, this time sending six hundred ships.

So successful was this Persian excursion that the eastern troops raided all the way to Athens. The Athenians, suddenly aware of what they were up against, sent an urgent message to the Spartans asking for help. The runner they sent went by the name of Pheidippides. His legs became the stuff of legend, carrying him as they did over 140 miles, the distance between Athens and Sparta, in just twenty-four hours. Upon arriving, he delivered his message.

The very manly Spartans refused to fight. Their oracles had a look at the omens and decided it would not be prudent to muster arms until the moon was full. (The name "marathon," inspired by the soon-to-be-fought battle, lives on as a reference to a long and pointless run that ends in pain and disappointment.) This refusal highlights an ironic fact of Spartan life: they did not particularly like to fight. The Spartans ruled over their slaves, the helots, with brutality and disdain. If the Spartans had to go away to fight, the slaves might take advantage of their absence and rebel.

If you asked a Spartan why he trained to fight all the time, he might answer that he had to be strong to keep his slaves in line. If you asked him why he had slaves, he might answer that he needed someone to do the work so he could train all of the time.

With no Spartan aid forthcoming, the Athenians turned to face the Persian aggressors at the plain of Marathon. The Athenian commander, Miltiades, ordered his hoplites into a Spartan-style phalanx with the mass of troops not at the center but at the edges. The Athenians charged, sacrificing the middle, but then pressed from the outside in on the Persians, who found themselves in an Athenian vice.

Most of the Persians bravely took off toward their ships, but while a large number escaped, a bunch also got stuck in the mud and hacked up by the Athenians, who captured seven Persian ships. By this time, a full moon loomed over the Aegean, and the Spartans felt like fighting. They came jogging up just after the battle ended.

## Dot 3: Xerxes

In 486, while raising both taxes and a new army in Persia, Darius got sick and died. His son, Xerxes, ascended the Persian throne. Xerxes announced his imperialist intentions by overrunning Egypt and then slapping around some revolutionaries in Babylon. By 484, he was sufficiently warmed up enough to avenge his father's humiliations in Greece.

The Athenians saw him coming and hammered together a fleet of ships and an alliance with Sparta, the latter going by the comic-bookish title of the "Hellenic League." By 480, the metaphorical chess pieces were in place—only Xerxes had about a million more rooks to play with than the Greeks did. The Spartans, however, controlled the center of the board, at a place called Thermopylae.

## Dot 4: The 300, er, 298 Spartans

Xerxes had to order his armies south in order to conquer the Greek heartlands, and this required that he march his troops south through a mountain pass. This would mean that his army would have to filter through the thin pass like sand moves south through an hourglass, with a large mass from the top trickling into another large mass at the bottom. The

CHAPTER FOUR

Spartans planned to position themselves at the stem of this hourglass, in the mountain pass, where only a small number of Persians could move at a time, and block the advance.

Spartan society, being selective, only produced about eight thousand adult male warriors at any given time. Even the headstrong Spartans could see that sending all eight thousand against Xerxes would risk ending their entire society. Instead, the Spartans selected three hundred soldiers, chosen because each had a male heir to carry on their line, and sent them to Thermopylae (translated roughly as the "hot gates"). Leonidas, one of the two Spartan kings, led the men to the pass. Two soldiers contracted some kind of eye disease on the route and had to drop out; one ultimately hanged himself, and the other died at a later battle.

The Spartan 298 actually led a Greek coalition force of nearly seven thousand men, and they all faced off against the uncountable masses of the Persians, but, to return to an earlier metaphor, the Spartan 298 consisted of knights and a king while the Persian army consisted only of rooks.

It is worth pausing here to note that one of the greatest tough-guy lines in ancient history came from this battle. When one Spartan warrior, Dioneces, was told that the Persians had enough arrows to block out the sun, he replied, "So much the better; we shall fight them in the shade." And they did.

The Persian hoard rushed into the mountain pass, but the Spartans slaughtered those who perpetuated the onslaught. Xerxes ordered his men forward into what became a meat-grinder as the 298 used their shields, spears, and a lifetime of brutal mental training to drive the Persians out of the pass.

On the second day, a Greek traitor told Xerxes about a pass around the hot gates, and the Persians then streamed upward, over the pass, and attacked the Spartans from behind. Caught in a vice, the Spartans fought on. Leonidas died, but on the third day the Spartan soldiers, worked into an exhausted frenzy, battled on to preserve his corpse from desecration. Eventually, the spears, shields, and bodies of the Spartans broke, but their spirits did not. Deprived of weapons, they punched and bit at the Persians.

They all died anyway. Xerxes had the corpse of Leonidas collected and then hacked off its head. Enraged, he ordered his army south. But it was smaller now.

## Dot 5: Salamis

According to Plutarch, who wrote much later than Herotodus, the Greeks argued about what the next step should be. Many wanted to plant an army in front of Athens to protect the city but feared annihilation if they fought the still-formidable Persian military. They retreated south instead. When the Persians stormed into the city and set the Acropolis on fire, the Athenians watched and smoldered.

One of the Greeks, Themistocles, switched sides. He went to Xerxes and told the enraged king that the Greeks, pinned in on the south, could be finished with a single swift stroke. Such advice fit Xerxes's mood perfectly, and he ordered his navy to make a full frontal assault through the narrow pass on the water at a place called Salamis.

It was like Thermopylae on water—as the Persians stormed through the pass, the Greek triremes (highly mobile war ships) destroyed Xerxes's fleet. The Persian sailors had never been taught to swim, and the waves battered them to death. As it happened, the Persian admiralty consisted entirely of Phoenicians and Xerxes ordered them all executed, thus ensuring that his only allies in the region abandoned him.

One can almost see the wry grin on the face of Themistocles; he had given the exact wrong advice to Xerxes. He knew that the proper plan of attack would have been to surround the Greeks with a blockade, and then tighten the noose over time until surrender became the only option. Xerxes had been tricked, and Themistocles continued his cunning ways by encouraging the Babylonians to revolt.

With all his plans, alliances, and navy destroyed, Xerxes retreated.

## Dot 6: The End

Xerxes went home but left his son-in-law, Mardonius, behind to engage in what amounted to a suicide mission. The Athenians gathered their strength and, led by Pausanius, a nephew of the lionized Leonidas, they crushed what was left of the Persian army at Plataea. Mardonius likely perished in the fight, but nobody ever found the body.

Supposedly, the other big final battle, at Mycale, took place on the same date. The Persian navy grounded their ships to fight on land, and their handful of Greek allies abandoned them. The Spartan and Athenian troops advanced and finished the once mighty Persian military off, driving them from Greece. The year was 479, and the Greeks had won their war against the Persians. They could now concentrate on fighting each other.

## Dot 7: The Peloponnesian War Begins

The Athenians rewarded Themistocles for his heroics by promptly ostracizing him. The rationale for the banishing was the same as it typically was: Themistocles had too great a reputation, and excessive reverence could quickly lead to tyranny. Themistocles did not help his cause by advocating that Athens turn itself into a tribute-collecting empire.

He went to, of all places, Persia. Supposedly, he charmed Xerxes by showing up and demanding the Persian king's ransom for turning himself in. Xerxes, likely in a better mood now that he was home enjoying all the comforts due to a king, provided refuge for his Greek enemy. Themistocles died there, either of old age (though he was only sixty-five) or due to poisoning.

Xerxes let his appetites get the best of him, and eventually his behavior (particularly the attention he paid to other men's wives) seems to have stirred up anti-Xerxian emotions among the Persians. One of his eunuch military commanders entered his king's bedroom and X'ed out the old tyrant.

Artaxerxes, the eighteen-year-old son of Xerxes, waited in the wings. As is often the case when a transfer of power occurs in empires, some of the outlying regions took the opportunity to rebel. Artaxerxes spent the next eleven years quelling these uprisings. The members of the Hellenic League, sensing that Persia wasn't what she used to be, questioned why they still had to be a part of the League at all, especially when membership required that they send tribute payments to the Athenians.

## Dot 8: Athens in Charge?

By 460 BCE the fracturing of the Hellenic League began. One of the Greek islands, Naxos, announced her disassociation with the League. The Athenians responded by laying siege to the islanders until they prudently changed their minds. Other regions followed the example of Naxos, and the Athenians responded in kind with additional force. Soon enough, fear of Athens, rather than the original fear of Persia, was the only thing knitting the League together.

Sensing the Athenian unpopularity, the Athenian king Pericles ordered the construction of walls from Athens to the port. This would allow safe passage for Athenians should they find themselves besieged by enemies. It would prove to be a prescient move by Pericles, as the Aegean political waters were becoming troubled.

With the Hellenic League on the verge of becoming an Athenian Empire, the weaker states appealed to the Spartans for help. Nothing in the Spartan background indicated that they would lie down while their rivals dominated the Aegean. In 457 BCE, the Spartans sent a force to the region of Boeotia, ostensibly because they had been called by the people of Doris in a nearby city-state.

They fought, of course, but no one won. In fact, after the draw it appeared for a moment that each side saw the senselessness of a drawn-out Greek civil war.

## Dot 9: Peace?

Eleven years after the battle at Boeotia, the Athenians proposed peace terms. It appears (no official record remains) that the Athenians offered to give some land up to the Spartans to stay out of each other's way. It amounted to a couple of bullies dividing up the block and agreeing not to pound on each other. The agreement, designed to last for thirty years, was called the Thirty Years' Peace. The name turned out to represent a wish rather than reality.

In this brief period of calm, Pericles orated to enthusiastic crowds and had the famous Parthenon built. Designed as a temple dedicated to the goddess Athena, the Parthenon would, in time, become a classroom of sorts where the homeless teacher Socrates would hold forth on the meaning of life. But first, war.

## Dot 10: It Begins

In addition to an Athenian and Spartan "empire," a lesser power called Corinth also existed at this time. The Corinthians remained separate from the peace agreements between the Spartans and Athenians, and when one

CHAPTER FOUR

of the Corinthian colonies requested Athenian aid in breaking away from Corinth, the Athenians, eager to tear off a chunk of a rival empire, obliged.

Problematically, the Corinthians had an alliance with the Spartans, and when the Athenians went to war with the former, the latter joined in. By now the collective Spartan ego had been piqued. The Athenian colonial machine had to be stopped, and a new generation of Spartans appeared eager to remind the Greek city-states that Spartan society produced warriors, not politicians and traders like their rivals.

Not all of the Spartans celebrated the outbreak of war. One of the Spartan kings, Archidamus II, warned his brethren that a war would ruin both states. Thucydides records him as a mournful and prophetic character, the only Spartan capable of admitting that Sparta could be anything but glorious.

The cautious words of Archidamus could hardly be heard above the enthusiastic shouts for battle that rose up from the Spartan warriors.

## Dot 11: Inglorious Plague

But the Athenians would not fight—at least not the way the Spartans wanted them to. Pericles ordered his citizens to retreat behind the newly built wall around the city. Let the Spartans have the countryside, he figured. Perhaps cowed by the reputation of the Spartans as nearly invincible infantry fighters, Pericles planned to use his navy to supply Athens while the Spartans uselessly fumed outside the walls.

Not a bad plan, in retrospect, given that Pericles knew nothing of germs. Packing all of those people and animals into an enclosed space, however, provided the perfect breeding conditions for viruses. Plague, described in all its phlegmy detail by the eyewitness Thucydides, ravaged the besieged citizens.

## Dot 12: Peace Again?

Back in Persia, Artaxerxes got drunk, falling into a stupor, and his half-brother killed him. This half-brother, in turn, was murdered by another half-brother. The latter named himself Darius II. The year was 424 BCE.

Three years later, the Athenians and Persians, exhausted and needing to gather crops, declared peace again. Nicias of Athens led the process.

One of the Athenians, Alcibiades, opposed the plan. Famously flamboyant, Alcibiades had a reputation for speaking with a lisp from a beautiful face. The man desired fame, something that could not be acquired during a period of peace.

For some reason, the Athenians listened to Alcibiades when he suggested a massive invasion of the Sicilian region of Egesta, far from the heart of Athenian power. The Athenians even made him co-admiral. Just before the 130 ships in the fleet set sail, someone (likely Alcibiades, who liked to drink and had a weird sense of humor) desecrated the religious icons on the ships.

Before the invasion got under way, a messenger ship showed up, and someone told Alcibiades he had to come home and stand trial for the stunt with the icons. Rather than face arrest and a trial, the Greek prankster took off and ran to the Spartans. One could only imagine how the Spartans reacted to such a character in their midst.

The Egestans took advantage of the confusion and soon had the Syracusians on their side. The other Athenian admiral, Nicias, sensed that the Aegean had become hot water and requested permission to retreat. The Athenian powers instead doubled down, sending another twenty-five thousand men.

It didn't go well. The Sicilian allies blocked the Athenian retreat, and all of the Athenian soldiers had to land in Sicily and try to walk to the other side. By the time the soldiers reached the Assinarus River, their throats burned with thirst. They piled on one another to get to the water while the Syracusians butchered them with swords and arrows. So thirsty were the Athenians that they fought with one another for the bloody water even during the carnage.

Nicias procured peace terms, one of which guaranteed his survival. The second he put down his sword, however, his enemies broke both the terms and him. Meanwhile, his co-admiral, Alcibiades, eagerly joined the Spartans in a full-scale invasion of the Athenian homeland. Unfortunately, Alcibiades managed to impregnate the wife of an important Spartan, an act that got him kicked out of his adopted home. He went to Persia, got some gold, and then asked the Athenians if he could come home and give them some of it. They said yes.

In 407 BCE, Alcibiades was given another fleet and directed it toward Sparta. The Spartan navy, led by an energetic new commander called Ly-

CHAPTER FOUR

sander, lay in wait. In the two years between 407 and 405 BCE, Sparta's navy ravaged the triremes of Athens. Alcibiades eventually ran out of friends, and his famous charm could not save him from the Persians, who set his house on fire and then stuck a spear in his guts.

The Athenian navy crushed, Lysander sailed to Athens and laid siege to it. The exhausted Athenians surrendered.

## Dot 13: Laughter Survived

How about a little humor? During the war, the great Athenian author Aristophanes penned the classic play *Lysistrata*. The plot involves Athenian women scheming to find a way to convince their husbands to stop all the fighting. The play contains themes that some might argue have not aged well, but surely everyone thought it was funny at the time.

Less funny were the Spartan surrender terms. The Athenians had to bring down the protective walls that Pericles had built to the port and give up any pretense of empire. Paralyzed by infighting, the Athenians could agree to surrender but put together no plan to follow through with Lysander's demands. Ticked off, the Spartan commander returned and created an oligarchy composed of thirty Athenian aristocrats (known, appropriately, as the Thirty).

The oligarchs liked this better than the old democracy and constructed a type of police state. Backed by Spartan soldiers, the Thirty ruled through terror, executing dissidents and alienating the masses. The Athenian people allied with Thebes and attacked the Thirty along with their Spartan allies. Lysander wanted to crush the rebellion, but by this time even the Spartans were sick of the whole thing and pulled everybody out of Athens. It was now 403 BCE, and once-mighty Athens, again democratic but still nearly destroyed, hoped for a new beginning. It would become an empire of thought.

## Connecting the Dots

While the Chinese faced internal threats, such as political fraction and disunity, in the era prior to the Qin Dynasty, Greek history was forged by an external threat: the Persians. The Persian desire to conquer Greece and establish a large-scale empire (defined, roughly, as a political system where an ethnic, religious, or nationalist "core" group rules over people they politically dominate) forced the Greeks into coalitions for defense. The breakup of these coalitions led to power struggles and civil war, and eventually to the creation of one of history's greatest conquerors.

That philosophy in the Western vein, including questions regarding the way in which humans should live and inquiries about the machinations of the world we do live in, should have developed in such a warlike environment is perhaps not entirely surprising, as philosophy often flourishes in chaotic circumstances.

## CHAPTER FIVE
# GREEK PHILOSOPHY

### Dot 1: Philosophy

The word *philosophy* translates to "love of wisdom." Greek intellectual achievement represents just this—a love of wisdom in all its forms. In the earliest days of civilization the amount of information available did not necessarily overwhelm scholars, and so no one sliced information up into different fields. Instead, mathematics, science, literature, and ethics all represented wisdom, and philosophy as a potentially scientific enterprise—in the sense that the philosophers asked questions about the make-up of the natural world—developed in the Greek region of Ionia, specifically in the city of Miletus. Three names, Thales, Anaximander, and Anaximenes, remain attached to this school.

### Dot 2: Thales

Thales does not have a life grounded in clear historical fact. Relatively unreliable sources put his birth date at 625 BCE, but who knows? Thales wondered about the fundamental "stuff" of nature. Many Greek thinkers maintained an obsession with this concept, which came in various forms. One question required the student to think about how many times one could cut up a fish before it ceased to be a fish (and became, say, an atom).

Thales thought that water made up the fundamental essence of the universe and that everything from ants to trees to stars represented

## CHAPTER FIVE

different manifestations of water. Water to Thales was what building blocks are to young children: malleable materials that can be broken down and reshaped into different forms.

### Dot 3: Anaximander

One of the students of Thales, Anaximander, ushered in a Greek tradition of sorts in which the students of great philosophers thoroughly disagreed with the positions of their teachers. (Alas, disagreeable students are still with us today.) Anaximander (who incidentally may have sketched the first map of the known world) believed that the universe could be boiled down to a fundamental piece, but nothing as easily definable as water.

Instead, Anaximander posited a universe composed of indefinable particles, but he proposed no clear material definition for his pieces. Whatever they were, they moved. These particles differed in their presentation depending upon the rapidity of their movement. The heat and the cold, for example, are different extrapolations of the original movement and define each other. At the human level of sensation, this moving mysterious stuff can appear as flames or mist, depending on the circumstances.

If this sounds a bit like the scientific concept of atoms in motion producing heat or cold depending on how much energy is infused (electricity heats up water and forces the atoms to dance), that's because it is. Anaximander seems to have intuited concepts that experiments later validated to some extent.

The possessor of an underrated intellect, Anaximander also seems to have intuited evolutionary theory. He speculated that life began in water and that energy from the sun sparked life in the mud, which then took the shape of little animals in the sea. These fish developed shells, which allowed for an embryonic stage in which humans could develop. Eventually, the fish burst onto land.

Anaximander might be credited with the first work of science fiction for this theory except that the core concept has proved one of the most stable notions in biology. Anaximander correctly noted that complex things come from simple origins, thus developing from the bottom up. This is not a small matter, and Western philosophers would, for centuries, forego this concept in favor of a top-down theory, which stated that complex things must be created by more complex things. Anaximander would later be validated by Charles Darwin.

## Dot 4: Pythagoras

The Milesian philosophers created an initial construct for what would later be called "natural philosophy" and evolve, by the late nineteenth century, into science. The Milesians asked questions about the fundamentals of nature but are not recorded as being interested in philosophy as an ethical guide. Historians of science sometimes refer to the Milesian quest for understanding as the "Ionian Enchantment." This poetic phrase nicely bottles up the quest to understand, scientifically, the universe and what it contains.

Pythagoras, born in about 570 BCE, is the first recorded philosopher in the West to have been driven off for his views. At the age of about forty, Pythagoras had to run away from a dictator named Polycrates. Pythagoras then made his way to southern Italy, where he took up teaching. At some point, the locals got upset with Pythagoras and his students ran him off. The old philosopher found refuge in a cave and eventually, unable to obtain food, died of starvation.

His students, however, continued to spread his teachings. One group of his followers focused on Pythagoras's ethical ruminations and called themselves the "akousmatikoi." Another group, interested in the philosopher's mathematical and scientific treatises, called themselves the "mathematikoi."

The thinking of the latter group proved to be the most interesting. As Terry Jones, the Monty Python comedian-turned-historian, has noted, Pythagoras apparently believed that numbers constituted the building materials of the universe. He may have come to this conclusion by asking, as all philosophers do, obscure questions. For example, why do certain combinations of musical notes sound pleasing while others do not? Pythagoras theorized that each note could be understood via a mathematical rationale—specifically, by the relationship of whole numbers to one another. Arrangements of pleasing whole notes created music that was in harmony.

Pythagoras formed this insight about music into an analogy to be applied for understanding the universe, theorizing that everything in the

CHAPTER FIVE

universe can be understood as a relationship between whole numbers. In this sense, Pythagoras may be the first to have engaged in the process of trying to understand the material of the universe through the analogies that humans have at our disposal.

Having discovered a pattern in music, Pythagoras mistakenly believed that the pattern must apply to everything. In fact, it was the triangle that destroyed Pythagoras's theory. A right-angled triangle with two equal sides cannot be made using units that are the same length (representing wholes). So died his theory.

## Dot 5: The Pre-Socratics

Beginning with Thales, the philosophers who thought and taught prior to Socrates are referred to as the "pre-Socratics," and among them were the Sophists. The Sophists asked questions and, in many cases, attempted to answer them. Most of these philosophers chose not to expound on their philosophies in clear, essay-like prose, instead opting to dole out their teachings in Homer-like hexameter poems or in the form of nebulous aphorisms.

Heraclitus saw information as being unified in an external reality called the *logos*, or word. Parmenides, one of the most controversial pre-Socratics, argued that one can only think about what actually exists and that the nonexistent defies the ability of language to describe it. To Parmenides, anything that exists must be eternally large and have no ending. The reason for this is that if something stops existing at a certain point in space, then it does not exist at all. Therefore, everything is made of one infinitely large and unchanging thing.

At this point, it's worth pausing to think of what Parmenides was doing. He created logical constructs and believed these forms of reasoning to be superior to reality. In other words, if reality did not seem to match his reasoning, then it was the reasoning that was more "real." Few people like epistemology (questions about how we know what we know) or metaphysics (a term invented later by Aristotle, which means thinking about thinking about things), but, historically speaking, when theorists draw attention to these two troubling modes of thought, great breakthroughs can be made.

Anaxagoras and Empedocles followed Parmenides and may have started the tradition of philosophers getting into trouble with the state. Anaxagoras suggested the sun might be a flaming rock rather than a god, an assertion that, along with his political activities, got him ostracized from Athens during the era of the Peloponnesian War.

Empedocles, a flamboyant character dressed in robes of purple, not only argued that the composition of the universe consisted of earth, air, fire, and water but also claimed to be a god himself. He got exiled, too, and probably died peacefully, but the better story has him, based on his conceit to be supernatural, hopping into a deep crater. Gravity always proves to be a harsh judge of god-like claims.

The last major name of the pre-Socratics is Democritus, who supposed that the universe must be made of tiny and unchanging particles. He called these atoms, a name later borrowed by physicists who detected, using scientific instruments, the actual existence of these particles. Well, maybe they did, if we define a fundamental particle as something made up of other particles in varying positions. Thinkers are still trying to solve the problem of understanding what happens in the world of the absurdly small, and how it is that these small particles, in the aggregate, make up the world that humans perceive. And so it goes on.

## Dot 6: The Big Three, Beginning with Socrates

The theme of philosophy in ancient Greece has been separated here from the political/military themes explored earlier, but it should be remembered that the two trends happened concurrently. The Big Three philosophers of the ancient world can be handily remembered by the acronym of SPA, standing for Socrates, Plato, and Aristotle. Socrates taught Plato, and Plato taught Aristotle (Aristotle subsequently taught Alexander the Great, but Alexander proved to be more interested in phalanxes than philosophy).

Combined, these three philosophers created a canon of thought that shaped the intellectual universe of the West up to the present. Socrates created not only an ethical guide to living but also an educational methodology that encouraged followers not to keep a system of thought as a whole, but rather to ask questions and follow the answers to conclusions. Plato established an ethereal notion of matter and set the philosophical

## CHAPTER FIVE

keystone upon which Christian theology was eventually built. Aristotle, well, he set forth a method of logical thought that would, in time, aim a hammer at Plato's keystone.

So far as we know, Socrates wrote nothing during his philosophical tenure. Everything we know about the great philosopher comes from the works of two authors: Xenophon and Plato. A friend of Socrates, Aristophanes, referred to the philosopher in his comedic plays and even created one, *The Clouds*, completely about Socrates, but these make no claim to historical accuracy.

Plato's works on Socrates consist of several dialogues between Socrates and various people, sometimes students and sometimes philosophical foes and foils. While it is unclear whether Plato's Socrates represents a real attempt to capture the historical man, or whether Plato chose to use Socrates as a fictional or semi-fictional character for passing on Plato's own ideas, the books themselves comprise the foundation of a classical education.

In the books *Protagoras*, *Gorgias*, and *Meno*, Socrates expounds his philosophy through ruthless dialogue, thus providing a stage for the Socratic method, which involves responding to questions or assertions with more questions. At first this might seem almost juvenile, and it can be if attempted by someone unskilled in philosophy, but when properly understood the methodology represents the pinnacle of the learning experience between pupil and teacher.

To begin, the teacher must know how to reason. And when he has reasoned to a conclusion of which he is certain, he merely invites his student to ask the same questions. Done properly, the student will follow each logical step until he ends up standing on the rhetorical hilltop.

The most famous and the most important of Plato's dialogues on Socrates involve his trial and execution by court-mandated suicide. These four works—*Euthyphro*, *Apology*, *Crito*, and *Phaedo*—detail the best-known drama in philosophical history.

By 399 BCE, Socrates had reached the age of seventy. He was a veteran of the Peloponnesian War and had no proper occupation. The upstanding citizens of Athens apparently lost patience with this aged, notoriously ugly, and homeless atheist who reveled in asking questions designed to call into question the very existence of knowledge itself, and they placed him on trial. Perhaps it was his charisma, or the fact that many youths show an inclination toward associating with counterculture figures, but Socrates had no shortage of students.

In *Euthyphro*, Socrates has been indicted by a man named Meletus (the dialogue indicates that Socrates and his accuser had yet to meet) and is casually making his way to the judicial proceeding in Athens. The reader learns of this through Socrates's conversation with Euthyphro, a young lawyer whom the old philosopher encounters on his trip. Socrates reveals that Meletus has accused him of corruption. The nature of this corruption has been well argued by classicists over the years.

The most common interpretation has it that Socrates, a freethinker, had been questioning the existence of the gods. The scholar I. F. Stone counters this idea by noting that Socrates publicly criticized Athenian democracy while praising the Spartan system, and this at a time when the Athenians had just lost a brutal war and endured the tyranny of the Thirty. Socrates's cause was not helped by the fact that the shenanigans of one his most famous pupils, Alcibiades, had helped the Spartans to win the war. Another, Critias, had tyrannical tendencies but died before the famous trial of his teacher.

Anybody with parents who raised him or her right knows that two topics always stir up trouble and are therefore to be kept out of polite conversation: religion and politics. Socrates refused to stop talking about either subject, and his questions threatened to cut the already fragile social threads holding Athenian society together.

In *Euthyphro*, Socrates spends very little time discussing his own circumstances and instead noses his way into his young walking companion's business. Euthyphro, it turns out, comes across Socrates while on the way to his own legal proceeding, where he intends to star as prosecutor pursuing a murder case against his own father. This lawyer seems to believe his actions are virtuous, until Socrates requires that his companion define "virtue," at which point the young lawyer finds that the old man has him in an epistemological headlock.

Socrates verbally shakes the man with question after question until, finally, Euthyphro, no doubt speaking for thousands of new philosophy students over the years, states that he cannot be sure of the truth. After a long time, Euthyphro finally breaks free, not with a superior logical argument, but by crying the equivalent of "uncle" and saying that he has to start moving or he'll be late.

CHAPTER FIVE

This dialogue contains all things Socratic: calmness in the face of persecution, an overwhelming interest in finding the truth, philosophical questioning/harassment, and finally a tacit admission that nothing can be truly known. Socrates loved to ask people to take the same logical steps that he did, only to lead them into a metaphysical wilderness known as a paradox. He may not have wanted everyone to live there with him, but he wanted to make sure they knew it existed.

## Dot 7: The Apology and Death

Three men, Anytus, Lycon, and Meletus, brought the charges against Socrates and the old man came before an Athenian jury of five hundred. The *Apology* features Socrates doing everything but apologizing. Instead, he bats Meletus around with rhetorical ease and in the process showcases the central tenets of his philosophical system.

Meletus mostly accuses Socrates of atheism, or disbelieving in the gods. Furthermore, Socrates faces the charge of teaching his methods to others and making the weaker argument seem stronger! Socrates, typically, replies that he is no teacher and merely spends his time expounding on topics. If people within earshot hear him and ask questions or make comments, then how can he be to blame?

The whole *Apology* features as a rhetorical masterpiece, but the jury finds Socrates guilty anyway, by a vote of 220–280. The only show of emotion that the philosopher allows himself is a statement that the verdict only comes from the high esteem in which the jurors hold Anytus and Lycon, and not because of the wretched rhetoric of Meletus. Socrates then famously states that a life lived without self-study is not worth living.

When asked what his punishment should be, Socrates suggests a fine. The jury instead convicts him to death, which in Athenian society involved drinking a poison called hemlock. Unconcerned, Socrates merely notes that age would do the job just as well if the jurors can wait. Either death brings eternal sleep, in which case he will rest, or it brings an eternal change; neither prospect is to be feared.

I. F. Stone, in particular, has written that the whole scene makes little sense in the context of typical Greek life. Playwrights had been joking about Socrates and the gods for years, and the polytheistic Athenians hardly appear, from the historical record, to have been religious fanatics. Maybe Socrates had not changed, but Athenian society, exhausted by the Peloponnesian War and the tyranny of the Thirty, had lost its sense of humor. Socrates, the opponent of everything, no longer seemed so harmless.

In *Phaedo*, Socrates meets his death. This dialogue showcases the calm approach of the ethical man toward dying. In the *Apology*, Socrates stated that nothing can harm a good man, and his conduct at the end of his life in this dialogue seems to uphold his philosophy. His students try to talk their beloved teacher into running away, as he is not seriously guarded. Socrates responds by spinning their arguments around, probing as to whether such an action could be ethically justified. One must comply with the laws, Socrates asserts, and when the time comes he takes the cup of hemlock and drinks it down while the surrounding students grieve his passing.

And yet he lives on.

## Dot 8: Plato

Present at the death of Socrates was one his finest students, Aristocles (428–347 BCE). Because he was a former wrestler, everyone referred to him by his nickname of "broad" or "broad shouldered," which in Greek translated to "Plato." With his teacher gone, Plato abandoned Athens, and then, after traveling to no one knows where, he returned to establish the Western world's first university, called the Academy.

The ideas displayed in Plato's voluminous writings cannot be given justice in summary, but he is best known for the Socratic dialogues described above. His work on governmental theory, divided into ten books, is called *The Republic*. Through these works Plato argued that society should be governed by "philosopher kings" trained specifically in the art of reason. Plato distrusted the semi-literate masses, and therefore democracy. Reason, he believed, should be the major driving force in decision making, and therefore those who had mastered the art of reason should be in political control.

The single idea most attributed to Plato involves the analogy of the cave. In the seventh volume of *The Republic*, Plato compares those unfamiliar with philosophy to people chained to the floor in a cave. Plato asks

CHAPTER FIVE

his readers to imagine a fire burning behind the people in the cave so that shadows form on the wall. If these prisoners never see anything but the shadows, they will mistake these shades of reality for what is actually real.

This sets up the mind for the understanding of Plato's complex philosophy, which purports to deal with unseen realms that are more real than the everyday reality experienced by people. Think of a triangle. Everyone learns that triangles can be dissected and understood by certain geometric theorems. The same is true of circles or any other shape, and mathematicians work with perfect shapes. However, if someone tries to actually draw a perfect right-angle triangle or mathematically precise circle, she would see that, while she had some concept of what a precise geometric shape should look like, actually making such a shape appear in the tangible world is impossible.

So what is more real? The image of the shape and the mathematical concepts derived from it, or the actual shape itself drawn before you? To Plato, the perfect circle or triangle must exist in another realm, and all of the triangles and circles that appear in this world are but imperfect shadows of the perfection. Things are judged to be beautiful, or just, or ethical, based upon how closely they match up with the real object in the other realm. Things are judged to be ugly, unjust, or evil depending upon how far they are away from the perfect object.

We can see now that Plato's philosophy amounts to a linguistic game. We have definitions and real objects that sometimes meet those definitions and sometimes do not, and Plato had no understanding of how things might evolve. One can see why Plato's philosophy would be so endearing to Christians later on, as the concept of this world being an imperfect shade of a perfect world, and of people in this world being imperfect copies made in the image of a perfect creator, fits nicely with embryonic Christian theology.

Plato's student Aristotle disagreed. And, in some ways, all philosophical and theological arguments to be developed in the future would have their roots in this argument between the philosophical titans of Greece.

## Dot 9: Aristotle

Aristotle entered Plato's Academy at the age of seventeen. Since he came from a wealthy family, Aristotle did not have to worry about making a living, and so he spent the next twenty years learning and teaching. When Plato died in 347 BCE, Aristotle moved on.

Acting as perhaps the first polymath, Aristotle pursued learning in all the major philosophical regions, delving into literary theory, science, rhetoric, physics, and formal logic. He invented deductive logic, where one creates theories based upon the evidence, and also the syllogism. The syllogism, a formal logical construct often shown in the form of "if A = B and B = C, then A = C," gave codified rules to thought.

The physics of Aristotle invoked an original "unmoved mover" or "prime mover," something that pushed the universe into being. Later Muslims and Christians, enamored of Aristotle, would call this mover "Allah" or "God." The reasoning was simple: there had to be some first cause that pushed movement and the universe into being. (Some argue that Aristotle's reasoning is not very convincing, as it does not answer the question of what the first cause was, but rather introduces another question, such as: Where did the Prime Mover come from?)

Aristotle disagreed with Plato as to the realm of forms; he was, in fact, a materialist. This meant that he believed everything in the universe had to be made of some material. Tell Aristotle that you saw a ghost, and he likely would have replied that if you saw the ghost, it must be made of something that light can bounce off of, or else it is self-luminescent—either way, the ghost would be made out of some kind of tangible material.

Aristotle got a few things wrong, writing that the objects in the solar system revolved around the Earth and creating a logical construct about motion that failed, eventually, to hold up to experimental scrutiny. Historically, Aristotle is as important for what he got wrong as he is for what he got right, for it would be the act of breaking away from Aristotle's physics that would give weight to experimental results over the authority of the ancients.

Oh, and he tutored Alexander the Great, but he seemed to have little impact. Aristotle was a great thinker and Alexander a great doer.

## Connecting the Dots

With Socrates, the Western world was given its most recognizable philosophical character. Socrates did not deal in opaque treatises about the natural world, but rather interested himself in how to live. Plato's

# CHAPTER FIVE

ethereal philosophy, his construct of a world of perfect forms, established philosophical principles that would meld eventually into theology. Aristotle's disagreement, his insistence on materialism and faint argument for a Prime Mover, created a chasm in the early Greek world of thought. Plato and Aristotle would face off again in the medieval world, and the friction between the two conceptual frameworks would spark the fire of the scientific method.

## CHAPTER SIX
# ALEXANDER'S ERA

### Dot 1: Phillip of Macedon

The Peloponnesian War depleted the energy of both Athens and Sparta, leaving room for other Greek city-states to achieve dominance. One of the northern city-states, called Macedonia, proved to have the energy to supplant the once great societies to the south. Phillip of Macedon, the first king of note from the area, proved to be a brilliant military innovator.

The Egyptians captured Phillip when he was a young man and imprisoned him. While there, Phillip learned of military tactics, such as the use of catapults, battering rams, movable towers, and piled earth (for climbing over city walls), hitherto unheard of in the Greek military world. Phillip also conceived of an expanded phalanx, made up of sixteen men, all of them carrying pikes.

Eventually, Phillip became a regent for a young king, but then his regional conquests made him powerful enough to be crowned in his own right. With his power consolidated and his military updated, Phillip looked southward, to Athens. One of the famous statesmen and orators of the era, Demosthenes, tried to warn the Athenians about Phillip, but no one really listened. A nine-year war, taking place between 355 and 346 BCE, ended with Phillip's conquest of Greece, and he even presided over the famous pass at Thermopylae.

J. M. Roberts has written that with Thermopylae and the other legendary Greek sites under Macedonian dominion, classical Greek civilization had ended. It was also the end of Phillip. One of his servants, for

# CHAPTER SIX

unclear reasons, stabbed him and then, while running away, tripped and was murdered himself by onlookers. Phillip died, and power passed to his twenty-year-old son, who had imbibed his father's passion for conquest. He went by the name of Alexander.

## Dot 2: Alexander the Great

As a youth, Alexander had studied under Aristotle, but the great philosopher seemed to have little effect. The only intellectual exercise that Alexander seems to have engaged in came from reading the *Iliad*, which the great conqueror allegedly placed under his pillow when he slept. It is easy to see the influence that the bloody book, including elegant poems about slaughter, had on Alexander.

Alexander's father tested him when he turned eighteen by placing him in charge of a division during one of the wars against a rival Greek city-state. Alexander performed so well that he may be described as a phenom, someone who displayed heroic gifts at a young age. After Phillip's death by assassination, rumors abounded that Alexander had engineered his father's murder, but history offers no verdict and people have been gossiping about Alexander for well over two millennia.

When Phillip died, Alexander ascended to power, and when the newly conquered city of Thebes revolted, Alexander bared his teeth. His troops crushed the revolt, then instilled terror in the population. Now an emperor in possession of his father's innovative military machine, Alexander eyed his next conquest. Well, he *was* Greek, so he might as well have a go at the Persians.

By 334 BCE, Alexander and his troops crossed into Anatolia (roughly modern-day Turkey). Young and hot headed, Alexander led his troops and overextended himself, which resulted in his being encircled by a contingent of Persian soldiers. His recklessness got him into trouble—and it also got him out, as Alexander, like a Greek superhero, simply burst out of the trap and won the battle.

In 333 BCE, legend has it that Alexander encountered the famous Gordian knot, created five hundred years before by King Gordius. (His son, Midas, became the subject of one of the world's most famous myths about greed and its destructiveness—Alexander would have done well to have read it.) The knot tied a grave marker—a wagon, in this case—to a large pole.

The Gordian knot served as a precursor to the old "sword in the stone" myth featuring a young King Arthur. The person who undid the knot, it was foretold, would rule Asia. Alexander either managed to untie the knot or, and this fits his style better, merely hacked the rope to pieces with a sword. Sometimes one must improvise on the way to attaining one's destiny.

Then the Persians fought back, often by employing mercenaries hired from the Greek population. In 333 BCE Alexander marched into Syria to face off against his nemesis, the Persian emperor Darius III. The battle proved to be a match between subtlety and brute force, with Darius gambling on a defensive strategy designed to take advantage of his Macedonian rival's aggressiveness. For poor Darius, it was like trying to trick a hurricane; he was overwhelmed by Alexander's army and personality. The great conqueror himself led the charge that caved in the Persian front's left flank. Darius ran away.

Master of the Mediterranean now, Alexander moved on to Egypt. He may have been driven by the desire to master the known world, or it could have been that his restive troops demanded conquest. Many of history's best-known warlords, from Alexander to Genghis Khan, more or less *had* to fight. Their troops depended upon the spoils of conquest for their pay, and they might overthrow a peaceful ruler in favor of one with a temperament better suited for war.

The Egyptians greeted Alexander as a pharaoh-cum-god and named one of their most important cities after him. Unsatisfied, Alexander desired the total destruction of Persia. By then Darius III had recovered from the initial failure of his campaigns, and he taunted Alexander with a new army he'd constructed in Mesopotamia near the Euphrates. In 331 BCE, Alexander moved to finish his rival in the rematch.

The two armies, unequal in size (Persia's fielded many more men), met at a place called Gaugamela. Battles cannot necessarily be described as clashes between the will of commanders, as the chaos of the fight presents too many random possibilities. But the comparisons between Alexander, who rode at the head of his armies and refused a night raid because it lacked glory, and Darius III, who cowered at the back behind

CHAPTER SIX

his soldiers, make it tempting to attribute the causes of the Persian loss to a lack of royal willpower.

Whatever the analysis, Alexander led a force that rolled up the Persian left flank, then drove a hard blow the solar plexus of the Persian infantry. Darius again retreated and the Macedonians routed the sad remnants of his army.

No one has ever been so cloaked in martial glory, but one cannot be both a god of war and just one of the guys. Alexander's men adored him because he fought with them and drank with them. (Plutarch tells of how Alexander refused a helmet of water on a desert march because there was not enough for everyone—and his men loved him for it.) But now, with his fame growing, Alexander claimed Hercules and Achilles as his ancestors. Alcohol and megalomania ate away at Alexander's health and psyche. He ordered the execution of his right-hand man, and he pinned his friend (and possibly lover) Clitus to a wall with a spear through the torso.

It was never enough. More territory had to be conquered, more reputation had to be acquired, and more glory feasted upon. In 326 BCE, Alexander took his troops to India. The Indians rode battle elephants into war and killed enough members of Alexander's army at the Battle of Hydaspes that his troops refused to listen to Alexander's exhortations to continue on. He may have been considered a god, but his troops would rather face his wrath than fight any more elephants.

While retreating, Alexander kept fighting, but his phenom days now lay behind him. Alexander had passed thirty, and his ability to defy the statistics of battle disappeared. One of his enemies inflicted a life-threatening wound. He marched on through the desert and in 325 BCE arrived in Babylon. Either he got drunk and died or the infections in his many wounds got to him. His corpse was well scarred.

## Dot 3: His Death and the Dissolution of Empire

No less than twenty-five cities are named after Alexander, the most notable being Alexandria in Egypt. After the birth of Islam, nearly nine hundred years later, Muslims would revere Alexander as a pre-Mohamedan prophet. No one could conceivably fill the man's sandals, and it did not help that he had died without naming a successor.

# ALEXANDER'S ERA

Imagine for a moment that the spears Alexander's men carried were metaphorical pencils, connecting the "dots" of the ancient world. Most of the great non-Chinese civilizations, including the Athenian, Egyptian, and Indus River Valley communities, were now connected into a unified empire, where trade and ideas could spread, synthesize, and, thanks to the more widespread dissolution of literacy and paper, be stored in a central database (which used to be called libraries). Fittingly, the greatest center of learning to develop after Alexander grew in the city named after the ancient world's greatest connector.

Alexander died surrounded by four generals: Ptolemy, Seleucus, Lysimachus, and Cassander. The four of them segmented the empire into separate regions and doled out a few of the smaller areas to four junior generals. Ptolemy got both Alexander's body and Egypt, arguably the best chunk of real estate. Predictably and promptly, the generals went to war with one another, and by 301 BCE they ended up with a three-way division of the spoils between the big three of Lysimachus, Seleucus, and Ptolemy.

Historians refer to post-Alexandrian era of Greece as the Hellenistic Era, since the Greeks called themselves Hellenes. In the post-Alexander era in the West, a new group of philosophers would generate novel schools of thought and come very close to creating a scientific method. In India, a warlord likely found his inspiration from Alexander.

## Dot 4: Indian Buddhism

In the 500s BCE, a warrior-caste Hindu named Siddhartha Gautama became unhappy with his relatively comfortable upbringing. He abandoned his home and took on the life of an ascetic for seven years, but then became a teacher. Gautama (now known as the Buddha) concerned himself with the cause of suffering and eventually concluded that the single cause of all suffering was desire. If one desired a loved one who had died, or desired an object one could not afford, this caused suffering. If one could rid oneself of desires, then suffering would go away.

The Buddha used yoga and other techniques to purge the body of fleshly desires. The ultimate goal of the Buddhist was to attain a state of being known as *Nirvana*. The concept is difficult to translate, but it seems to indicate a position where someone has broken out of the cycles of daily life. A teacher who has reached Nirvana, or come near that state, and returns to help others is known as a *bodhisattva*.

An atheistic religion, Buddhism emphasized neither faith nor deities. The Buddha did not declare himself a god, nor did he claim to speak for a god. The idea at the center of Buddhism was that a practitioner could attain a state of being over time. Buddhism appealed to women and to the lower-caste Hindus, many of whom might have been dissatisfied with the caste system.

While Buddhism retained the Hindu concept of reincarnation, it did not force practitioners into a social class for life as Hinduism did. Buddhism would in time influence many Asian cultures, but in India the religion would especially appeal to Ashoka, the third Mauryan emperor.

## Dot 5: Chandragupta's India

Alexander and his army spent very little time in India, wisely retreating as they did after the sight of the battle elephants (remember, one of history's greatest lessons is *always run away from battle elephants*). Yet it is possible that he infected an Indian warlord named Chandragupta with the conquest virus. At the very least, Alexander's idea of military conquest and the creation of empire must have given Chandragupta a few ideas.

Some historians have taken to calling Chandragupta the "Indian Julius Caesar," but John Keay, an eminent historian of Asia, has argued that it would be better to call Caesar the Chandragupta of Rome, given their chronological order. Not much is known about Chandragupta; no immortal battles are etched next to his name. Yet he apparently led armies that conquered territory stretching from the Bay of Bengal to the Arabian Sea, meaning that Chandragupta controlled the trans-Indian trade route. The domains under his control became known as the Mauryan Empire. One Greek traveler, Megasthenes, visited the Mauryan Empire and remarked on the relative tolerance of Indian society, the impressive imperial palaces, and, of course, the elephants.

Here's where it gets strange—sometime later in his life Chandragupta turned power over to his son and adopted a religious outlook known as Jainism.

Hindu doctrine expressed the interconnectedness of life. Hindus often refuse to eat meat because to do so would destroy another life—hence the emphasis on vegetarianism. One branch of Hindu thought, known as Jainism, stresses the respect of life to the point that an individual seeks to harm nothing. Supreme practitioners of Jainism eventually stop eating not only meat but also plants, and then stop moving so as to avoid harming even insects or other organisms. Chandragupta, apparently, adopted this outlook and stopped ruling, stopped eating, and eventually stopped breathing. He died in 356 BCE.

## Dot 6: Ashoka

Chandragupta's son, Bindusara, didn't do much, but *his* son, Ashoka, left behind some of India's first recognizable documents of a sort. Like Alexander, Ashoka seemed interested in merging the East and the West. He's a legendary figure, and, like all ancients, it's hard to see reality through the mist of myth. Buddhists have a tradition of relating how bad they were before finding religion, and it was said that Ashoka killed ninety-nine of his brothers and visited a nasty version of the afterlife before returning to create a torture room based on his otherworldly encounters.

He took power in 268 BCE and eight years later took part in the whole conquest thing by having a province called Kalinga crushed. One hundred thousand men died, and another hundred and fifty thousand were deported. These numbers are recorded on one of the Fourteen Rock Edicts, large stone pillars that Ashoka had planted around his kingdom. As a general rule, skepticism guides the historian when it comes to the numbers of men involved in battles, and especially the number of vanquished, because conquerors might have padded the numbers in order to inflate their glory and boast.

But Ashoka was not boasting; instead, these numbers were recorded for the purpose of sharing the depths of his remorse. The concept of *Dhamma*, a gentle philosophy of life, remains inscribed in the stone. What to make of this? Here we have Ashoka, after a great conquest, not bragging, but more or less saying that all of the suffering that the conquest required as payment represented too high a price. Such humility (sure, he referred to himself in the third person and called himself the *Beloved of the Gods*, but still . . .) appears nowhere else in the blood-soaked annals of the ancient world.

With the support of Ashoka, Buddhism flourished and spread throughout India. Roads were built and Ashoka commanded the planting of trees so that animals and men might find a little shade on their journeys. But Dhamma proved to be too weak of a string to hold India together, and after Ashoka's death, the people of the subcontinent fell back into their old habits. Caste, not empire, remained the focus of loyalty for most people. In 185 BCE, the last of the Mauryan emperors was murdered, and the dynasty, already frayed, collapsed.

India's factionalism then swallowed history; independent kingdoms formed, and nomads stormed down from the north. Buddhism morphed from its atheistic roots into a religion where the Buddha figured as a god rather than a teacher, and Christianity arrived in the north around the first century CE. A dark age may not have quite fallen, but this period gives off little light for the historian. India's narrative would not emerge from the chaos until the arrival of the Gupta Dynasty.

## Dot 7: Egypt's Library

Alexander's general Ptolemy took control of Egypt, the region more or less in the center of the newly united empire. (Ptolemy's line of successors would control the ancient state for nearly three hundred years, and the last of the Ptolemaic rulers would be none other than Cleopatra, Queen of the Nile.) Persian gold from the newly conquered regions flooded into the area around the Nile, causing what had been, for a long time, an intellectual and economic desert to bloom in full.

Although Alexander's conquest state shattered rapidly upon his death, the lines of communication and trade established as a result of his connections allowed for a greater flowing of information. Crucially, this information could now be recorded and stored. Legend has it that Alexander conceived of the first library. When Ptolemy ordered the creation of a library and museum, the world had yet to see anything of this scale.

A library grew at Alexandria, which came to be recognized as the best place to get an education. A reported 100,000–400,000 scrolls lay stacked on top of one another in what we could now describe as the world's first major database. Three or four dozen men, known as *synodos*, had access at any given time.

In the philosophical solar system of the Hellenistic world, the library acted as the sun, providing a gravitational pull that attracted the best minds of the day into its orbit. Furthermore, it illuminated many previously unfound concepts in its light. Those minds included Euclid, Aristarchus, Ptolemy, and especially Archimedes.

## Dot 8: The Charakitai

The word *charakitai* translates to "scribblers," but the better definition is "translator." Ptolemy, like his successors, wanted to combine the knowledge of the known world. He therefore paid these translators to copy the world's knowledge into Greek. One of the best known of the scribblers was Eratosthenes (276–196 BCE); he worked out the interconnectedness of the oceans in the world and perceived that India might one day be sailed to by going west across the Atlantic, an idea that Columbus would try out about sixteen hundred years later.

Eratosthenes used an inventive method of measuring shadows to determine the circumference of the planet and came pretty close to the twenty-six-thousand-mile number currently measured by scientists. He also created the time line and put the most significant events of the ancient world on it. This may sound insignificant, but it might be possible to trace the Western concept of progressive history to this man. Other cultures, particularly the Chinese, developed a circular concept of history. The time line fits better with the concept of technological progress.

## Dot 9: Euclid

Geometry may predate Euclid, but before him no one had collected and formalized geometric concepts into a system. Euclid, who lived at the time of Ptolemy in the period right after Alexander's death, stood on the shoulders of giants at Alexandria and systematized concepts of mathematics that stretched back to the time of Thales.

The book he produced, *Elements of Geometry*, accomplished nothing less than the explanation of a rigid and numerical system of logic. Moving in an evolutionary manner from the simple to the complex, Euclid established the three major concepts of geometry: axioms are statements that require no proof, theorems are developed on axioms, and then arguments and conclusions are structured on top of the theorems.

This may sound simple or even boring, but therein were contained all of the basic rules of logic, and therefore the concept of the logical fallacy.

CHAPTER SIX

If one, for example, states an axiom as a conclusion, this is called "jumping to a conclusion" or sometimes "begging the question." One cannot conclude with an untested axiom, or else one merely assumes, on faith, the conclusion. This is backward reasoning, or starting with a belief and then constructing a premise and argument that leads to where you started.

Tautologies, or circular forms of reasoning, involve saying merely that A = A, just because it is. Variations of Euclidian logic can be found everywhere in history. Science, for example, develops the original axioms or postulates for an argument based upon experimental evidence. The twentieth-century philosopher Bertrand Russell has noted that the Declaration of Independence declares that "All men are created equal" and proclaims this "self-evident," just as many axioms are. In practice, Euclid applied universal rules of logic and argument to shapes.

For the Greeks, no branch of thought proved more directly relevant than geometry, since this dealt with the type of squared patterns useful for making farming plots. Thinkers could turn shapes on the page into monumental forms of architecture and develop artwork with it. Geometry, however, limited Greek thought to that which exists in the real world. They never conceived of the mathematics of the infinite or the void. They never thought of the zero or any of the mathematical forms, such as decimals and negative numbers, that developed as a result of that concept. That would come later, with the Indians.

## Dot 10: Aristarchus and Ptolemy

One of the scholars at Alexandria, Aristarchus of Samos, posited a heliocentric (sun-centered) universe. Conversely, Claudius Ptolemy did his best thinking between 127 and 151 CE, well after the great age of the library. Ptolemy wrote a work that the Arabs later called the *Almagest*, which outlined the principles of trigonometry.

His book argued that circles and the angles of triangles have an intimate connection, and this connection can be superimposed and stretched onto the night sky. The system he developed, known simply as the Ptolemaic system, involved a complex argument for the cycles of the stars. He did not believe the Earth moved because, under his geometric concept, this would change the relation of the stars to one another, which is not what astronomers observed.

ALEXANDER'S ERA

Aristarchus, the original Alexandrian scholar, was, of course, right but also inconveniently dead. He had been gone for nearly four hundred years. The Ptolemaic system fit the religious sensibilities of both the later Muslims and the Christians, and it would reign as the universal paradigm until Copernicus, with his troublesome philosophy, and Galileo, with his meddlesome telescope, both dusted off the heliocentric theory and eventually proved it with evidence.

## Dot 11: Engineering

One engineer from the era, Philo, apparently invented a series of machines to spread messages via secret code and made pumps that ran on air and with chains. He also presaged the steam era by developing machines that might fairly be called robots, which operated under steam power for entertainment purposes.

At the turn of the twentieth century, an underwater diver found an astrolabe made during the Hellenistic era. Several decades later it was rebuilt and turned out to be a clockwork timepiece/astrological navigator device—pretty impressive stuff for people who lived before modern scientific instruments.

## Dot 12: Archimedes—Part 1

Archimedes (287–212 BCE) lived at the island of Syracuse but studied extensively at Alexandria's library. Almost without argument, Archimedes emerges as the preeminent intellect from the Hellenistic Era, and his mind ranks among history's finest. His story intersects with that of Rome. Archimedes developed a way to conceptualize huge numbers by trying to imagine how to count all the grains of sand in the world. In order to do this, he developed the idea of noting numbers by different powers but mathematically. In addition to this achievement, he showed that the distance that weight is from the fulcrum point affects the ratio of weights. He likewise proved that all objects have a center of gravity.

He accomplished all of this, and yet he ran around naked in the street *once*, and that's all anyone remembers him for. While mentally working on the problem of fluid displacement, Archimedes got into a bathtub prepared for him; when the water sloshed out the side, he realized that

## CHAPTER SIX

his weight had pushed the fluid upward because there wasn't enough to handle his bulk. Excited, he jumped up and ran around in public shouting, "Eureka!" which is Greek for "I've found it!"

The Romans remembered him differently—as a man whose very mind constituted a weapon. The Hellenistic era Greeks managed to get tangled up in the Punic Wars between Rome and the area of northern Africa known then as Carthage. The Roman boot, when it came, crushed the delicate flower that was Hellenistic thought. It is to the story of the Roman Republic that this narrative now necessarily turns. Archimedes will reappear in this narrative shortly, and his death will say much about the Roman effect on Western intellectual history.

### Connecting the Dots

Alexander restructured the world in a number of ways. By conquering all the way into India, he seems to have inspired Chandragupta to create an empire in the wake of the retreating Greek armies. And, by connecting the great ancient societies of the world, Alexander's empire provided the right kind of conditions for ideas to flow. Those ideas were written and compiled in the world's first major library at Alexandria.

Archimedes features as both an exemplar for the Hellenistic era of philosophy and an important connecting point between the history of Greece and that of the Roman Republic. As the Roman Republic grew in influence and power, it clashed with the other major Mediterranean empire of Carthage, which was in North Africa. Syracuse, and thus Archimedes, got caught up in this power struggle.

**CHAPTER SEVEN**
# ROME

## Dot 1: Names and Sources

To begin, let's clear up some of the semantic confusion. One word, *Rome*, is too often used to describe a civilization/empire that existed in some form for about two thousand years. Rome began as a kingdom, became a storied republic, and then, during the era of Julius and Augustus Caesar, morphed into an empire dominated by a succession of "Caesars" or emperors (who, in turn, were usually dominated by their soldiers).

After the time of Constantine in the early fourth century, Christianity overtook Rome's previously popular polytheism and the empire split into two. The western empire, fragile for reasons to be studied later, finally collapsed in 476 BCE, while the eastern empire lived on until 1453 and took the name of Byzantium, or the Byzantine Empire. It, too, is sometimes called Rome. Early on, however, Rome functioned as a republic, and it is the Roman Republic and its interactions with Greece and Carthage that serve our purposes here.

What we know about the Republic comes from just a few well-trod (and probably not very reliable) sources. There is Polybius (200–188 BCE), a Greek taken hostage by the Romans during the Macedonian Wars who wrote of their history. There is Cicero (106–43 BCE), the most famous of Roman senators and orators, whose letters, speeches, and works of philosophy made up a large part of what was once termed a classical education. He reported frequently on the crises of the later Republic. Livy (65 BCE–17 CE) recorded the most comprehensive history of the early Republic, but his sources come from the records of prestigious Roman families—his work details the infamous Punic Wars. Finally, there was Plutarch (40 CE–125 CE), whose life paralleled that of early Christianity (of which he makes no mention in his works) and who recorded what he knew about an ancient world that was several hundred years distant from his own life.

## Dot 2: Romulus and Remus

Rhea Silvia, an honored Vestal Virgin of the city of Alba Longa, became pregnant. This fact proved difficult to square with her title, and she defended herself by claiming that the cause of her pregnancy was no mortal but a god. Her twins, when they came, were given the names of Romulus and Remus. The king, Amulius, had usurped the throne from a man named Numitor, and Rhea was the daughter of the royal who had been wronged; Amulius had made her a Vestal Virgin to avoid the possibility of her having any children who might challenge him. He ordered that the babies be placed in the Tiber River to die of exposure.

The river flooded and supposedly not only washed the babies up on shore but also drowned the pups of a now mournful she-wolf. She responded to the cries of the boys and the ravenous babies suckled at her teats, a metaphor indicating that the boys gorged themselves on the milk of a wolf and absorbed wolfish instincts.

These two young rakes grew up unaware of their parentage and roiled around with low-society types for years, until Remus got into trouble and was brought before Numitor for judgment. The old man recognized his grandson and raised a rebellion against his rival Amulius. Romulus aided the rebellion, and the old man, trying to avoid his fate by killing a couple of babies, ended up being strangled by his own destiny. With Amulius dead, Romulus and Remus decided to found a city of their own.

That's what Plutarch tells us, anyway. 753 BCE is the recorded year of the Roman foundation, just twenty-three years after the original Greek Olympics.

## Dot 3: From Kingdom to Republic

Being brothers, Romulus and Remus naturally fought. For some reason, Remus hopped over the city walls that his brother was having built and died. Romulus, from whom Rome takes its name, appealed to people by offering sanctuary inside the city, more or less guaranteeing that that he would attract people of a criminal sort. Almost everyone who accepted the terms were men. In order to get women, they merely raided the town of Sabine and stole a few. The modern tradition of carrying a bride over the threshold of a house on the wedding night dates to these kidnappings, symbolizing that the women were going in against their will.

Romulus married a Sabine woman and eventually made peace with the Sabines. At this point, he was considered a god-like figure and set about conquest. A gifted soldier, credited by one worshipful biographer with killing seven thousand men by himself in one battle (a bit much on the lie, even for a Roman king and demigod), he got cocky and became very religious. As he stood in the rain during a storm that blew up during a sacrifice, the senators stayed with him. Romulus disappeared when the storm did, and despite legends that he ascended directly to the heavens, it's more likely that the senators did away with him.

Seven kings followed him. The last with any real power went by the title of Tarquin the Proud. At that time, those who lived in poverty could not be in the army, so Tarquin kept them busy building temples and roads and the like to prevent revolution. Tarquin's son, Sextus, took advantage of his father's absence to commit a crime that ultimately destroyed the kingdom.

Sextus had developed an obsession with the beautiful wife of his friend. The woman's name was Lucretia, and Sextus failed in his efforts to woo her into becoming his mistress. In response, he promised to kill both her and one of her slaves, and then smear their memory with a sordid tale of adultery. The spoiled prince followed this up by sexually assaulting her. Psychologically shattered, Lucretia told her father and husband about the crime and then killed herself.

Even the people of Rome could not abide such a vicious act, and rebellion swept the city. Tarquin attempted to smash the uprising but failed, and his later attempts to reconquer the city with a compilation of allies fared just as badly. He had one last go at it at a battle at Lake Regillus in 496 BCE, but the Romans won again, and the old man gave up trying and went away to die. Thus did 244 years of monarchical rule come to an end.

The leader of the rebellions went by the name of Lucius Iunius Brutus. (Every man in Rome had three names—the name his family members called him first, the second being the name of his clan, and the third being a nickname. All daughters took a female variation of their father's first name. A Roman named Julius could have as many daughters as nature would allow, and all would be called "Julia.") Lucius's nickname "Brutus" was derived from the word *brute*, as in someone with a slow mind. Raised in Tarquin's royal household, the king's sons bullied the boy with sadistic glee.

Probably because Brutus was considered stupid, Tarquin made him his second in command. But Brutus may have been, above all things, a talented actor. In a society that punished those who were too obviously cunning, his perceived slow-mindedness may have saved him. At any rate, he somehow discovered the wits to lead a rebellion after Lucretia's assault.

After the Roman people dismissed Tarquin, they set up a sort of democracy whereby the army elected the leader; this person would serve for a single year, lest he become too powerful. As a further defense against tyranny, the elected person would share power with another. To describe this type of rule, the Romans used a farming metaphor and called the rulers *consuls* (to plow together), borrowing from a Latin term describing two oxen hitched to a plow.

## Dot 4: Outsiders

Rome's fragile republic immediately came under attack from the "barbarians" who attacked from Gaul (modern-day France). The Romans called the people of Gaul "Celts," which meant, roughly, "to strike." War chariots, iron spears, and shields have all been found in the graves of the Celts. These people multiplied quickly and saw Rome as a potential settlement for their overflow population.

They struck at the edges of the Republic, and Livy tells us that, in 501 BCE, the Romans elected a dictator who could respond quickly to outside invasions and provide protection. One of the principal philosophical challenges of democracy had already become apparent. To be free meant to be vulnerable, but how much freedom should be given up for safety?

## Dot 5: Patricians and Plebeians

In Rome, two distinct classes appear in the historical record. The patricians formed the upper class, and the word is derived from the Latin word *pater*, meaning "father." Everyone else fell into the category of plebeian, which simply meant they were not a patrician. The latter formed the masses, but the former controlled the best land and the important titles. The plebeians often owed the patricians money, and if they had to go and fight in a battle, they couldn't pay their taxes and ended up becoming debt slaves.

Livy details that this unfair situation became unbearable in 495 BCE, when a scarred and unkempt soldier delivered a fevered oratory against the system in the Forum. Debt slaves, hearing of his courage, revolted in the streets, and most of the Roman senators ran and hid. A few entered the Senate, but the debt slaves, like zombies in a horror movie, pushed in the doors and piled in through the windows. Surrounded, the senators passed a law exempting military personnel from debt slavery.

In 494, still dissatisfied, the plebeians organized a strike that in time became called the Plebeian Succession. The Senate responded by setting up judges known as tribunes, who could not be of the patrician class. These tribunes functioned as non-political judges, similar in a way to the American Supreme Court. It still wasn't good enough, and in 451 BCE the Romans decided to craft a written law code and nominated ten legislators to carve the law into writing.

Humanity no longer has a copy of it, but the finished work of the legislators became known as the Twelve Tables and was hung in the Forum for public display. While the laws decidedly did not proclaim equality among the classes, they did spell out that the plebs possessed certain rights that the patricians could not just trample. Still, women had to have guardians, "deformed" babies were to be executed, and intermarriage between the plebs and the patricians remained illegal. It's instructive that these laws were considered improvements.

## Dot 6: Skyfall—the Gauls Again

In 396 BCE, a tribe of Celts (also called Gauls) struggled to find a place to live within the Roman territory. For about a hundred years, the Celtic population had grown, and the Celts continued to migrate south in search of extra land. As the Celts moved toward some of the major cities in the Republic, a plebeian tried to warn those in charge of the menace the Celts presented, but no one would listen to someone of his lowly status. They should have.

CHAPTER SEVEN

Livy details the Celtic destruction of an over-proud Roman military contingent and the ensuing Celtic march to Rome. The Roman soldiers retreated to the walled capital while the Celts rampaged through the city. Witnesses remembered a scene both iconic and horrific, of rampaging barbarians burning and looting while screams and smoke hung overhead. Having looted the outlying areas, the Celts lay siege to the capital.

The besieged Romans learned that the Celts could be bought off from the citizens of a Greek colony who had done just that. The Romans raised a tremendous sum of treasure and offered it to the Celts if they would just go away. The Celts took the money and migrated back to the mountainous north. The impoverished Romans who wandered out of the capital surveying the ruins of their once proud city must have been overwhelmed by a single thought: *never again*.

## Dot 7: The Punic Wars

After the Gaulic conquest of Rome, fear seemed to govern Roman foreign policy. If the problem was that outsiders, or barbarians, threatened civilization, then the solution was to defeat these barbarians and civilize them, thus neutralizing any potential threats. Eventually, Rome's expansionist impulses would lead her legions into war with the other military power of the Mediterranean: Carthage.

Forming the foundation of Rome's empire, the Roman legion presented an awe-inspiring combination of rapid mobility, discipline, and cohesiveness. These attributes made the legions, and thus Rome's entire military, the most significant force of its time. At the top of hierarchy stood the commander, and though no one expected him to fight on the front lines, the troops did expect the commander to suffer the travails of military discomfort along with them. If the legions held Rome together, the bond between the soldiers and the commander held the legions together. In time, these personal bonds would undo the Republic, but that is a story for later.

Like a good boxer, the legions had only a handful of maneuvers, but they executed each swiftly and with precision. Commanders forced the troops to practice each maneuver until the concepts became drilled into the muscles and minds of the troops. Each Roman soldier felt a connection to his comrades, and each would share in any defeat. Roman discipline came in the form of decimation, a word that literally means to reduce something by a tenth. When a legion failed to perform well, the commanders executed one out of every ten soldiers.

The Roman soldiers faced tough adversaries, and the horse-riding soldiers of the east, under the banner of the Sassanid and Parthian Empires, inflicted some defeats on Rome. To the west, the Romans fought the Germanic and Celtic tribal warriors and mostly won, but not always. And then there were the Huns, who swept down to threaten Rome on more than one occasion. The city founded by children of the wolf was itself surrounded by wolves.

## Dot 8: Hamilcar and Hannibal Barca

By the second century BCE, Carthage in North Africa became powerful enough to threaten Rome's dominance of the Mediterranean. Between 264 and 241 BCE, the two powers battled to dominate the island of Sicily. Hamilcar Barca, Carthage's most significant commander, won all of his initial battles in Sicily, and especially a siege at Drepanum in 241, but a maritime catastrophe concluded the war for the Carthaginians.

Hamilcar negotiated safe surrender terms, but his soldiers, who had gone without pay, rebelled. Eventually, Hamilcar snuffed out the rebellion and invaded Spain, but he never threatened Rome. His second son, Hannibal, imbibed his father's passion for revenge against the Romans.

Oh, how Hannibal, born in 247 BCE during his father's war, hated the Romans. Hamilcar Barca taught his son to lead and fight. Hannibal honed his skills fighting in Spain as a young man, and by 219 BCE (after a slave killed his older brother, which transferred power to Hannibal) he felt ready to fight Rome. His soldiers attacked the city of Saguntum and then, with Rome's anger stoked, staged the ancient world's most notorious invasion.

Hannibal decided to cut out Rome's heart; to do so, he would have to invade. Rather than attacking from the south, Hannibal decided to take an army north and cross the Alps into Rome. The Romans counted on the seemingly impenetrable northern mountains to protect them, but Hannibal and his troops attempted the crossing nevertheless. Of course, they took elephants with them, but most of the unfortunate pachyderms died in the alien environment; the few that made it across no doubt terrified the Romans but likely had a negligible military effect.

CHAPTER SEVEN

The army did not do much better, and Hannibal left a significant portion of his force behind him in the teeth of the Alps. Once across the mountains, they proved strong enough to defeat a small force at Ticino River. Hannibal's legend spread, and Celtic barbarians melded with his forces.

The shock wore off quickly, and the Romans sent a force to check Hannibal's progress at the Trebia River in the north. The overconfident Romans attacked, and Hannibal caught them in a noose, crushing the sides of the Roman force and then sending his main attack force to hit the Romans from behind. The legions proved powerful enough to break through the encirclement, but this only allowed them to escape. Another brutal defeat in 217 BCE sent panic into Rome and caused the election of a dictator.

## Dot 9: Fabius Cunctator

The initial success of Hannibal so frightened the Roman people that they apparently became willing to give up their freedom for protection. Fabius Cunctator, a former consul now in his sixties, accepted a six-month term as dictator. Sensing that Hannibal's armies would overwhelm the Romans, Fabius inculcated a strategy of caution. He wanted to let Hannibal roam across Roman territory, while smaller divisions ripped away at the Carthaginian edges.

Such a strategy proved unpopular with the Romans, who were forced to watch as Hannibal and his men tore up their land. Besides, this was Rome, an empire based on military power. The Roman taste ran toward big set-piece battles. When one of Fabius's subordinates won a significant battle against Hannibal, public opinion tilted in favor of a large-scale showdown against the Carthaginians. When Fabius's six-month tenure expired, he was allowed to step down.

## Dot 10: Cannae

The Romans should have listened to Fabius. In 216 BCE Hannibal took over a supply station at a place called Cannae; this amounted to a direct taunting of the Romans. The Roman generals, caught up in war frenzy after Fabius's delaying tactics, attacked. On August 2, the Roman legions crossed a river and made ready for battle.

Typically, the Roman battle plan involved pushing against the center of the enemy lines, hoping to break the middle and then cause a rout. Hannibal anticipated such a bullish attack and put himself in the center to entice the Romans further. Hannibal deftly used the strengths of his coalition members (consisting of Libyans, Numidians, and Gauls, among others) and posted the horse riders at the flanks.

When the Romans pushed hard on the center, Hannibal's army flexed on the edges into a circle, and the Romans found themselves trapped in the middle. The resulting massacre remains etched in history as Rome's greatest military defeat. Hannibal seemed unbeatable after Cannae.

For some inexplicable reason, Hannibal did not move toward the city of Rome, instead choosing to linger in the countryside seemingly without purpose. In military history, this ranks with Adolf Hitler's failure to finish off the British and French troops when they were pinned against the English Channel at Dunkirk in 1940. No matter; Rome survived, if only through luck.

## Dot 11: Syracuse and Archimedes

At this point, Rome's expansionist narrative connects with that of the Hellenistic era. In 214 BCE, two years after Cannae, the Roman consul Marcellus sent troops into Syracuse to eradicate some slight opposition. The crackdown was prompted by a fear of rebellion, but the suppression of dissent actually caused the rebellion it was intended to prevent. The Romans arrested anyone accused of conspiracy against them, executing around two thousand dissidents.

A real rebellion promptly broke out. The ensuing battle for Syracuse might be titled "The Roman Military vs. the Brain of Archimedes." Archimedes, the theoretical math whiz who developed mathematical notation and water displacement theory, now turned his intellectual powers to the development of war machines. One of these machines seems to have consisted of a massive claw that swung out from the walls of Syracuse and could pick up and/or dunk invading ships. He may also have created a system of mirrors designed to intensify sunlight to burn holes in the invading ships of the Romans.

Cleverness rarely trumps brutality, and the Romans kept attacking. When the Romans burst into the city, one of the soldiers found Archimedes alone in a building. Some important math problem he'd scratched into the dirt absorbed the attention of the old philosopher, and not even an invasion could break his concentration. Upon seeing a reckless Roman soldier in the doorway, Archimedes could but utter a plea that his work not be erased before the Roman hacked him to death. Even Marcellus grieved at this pointless eradication of a singular genius.

## Dot 12: Fabius and Scipio

All of a sudden, Fabius Cunctator looked a little smarter. His prediction that a headstrong attack on Hannibal would lead to disaster had found vindication on the bloody fields of Cannae, and he was made consul again, this time for two years. Patience, he believed, would defeat Hannibal, and a policy of less aggressive military tactics was again implemented. Predictably, Fabius disapproved of the plan of General Publius Cornelius Scipio (later called Scipio Africanus), which involved invading Carthage at its heart while Hannibal remained in Rome.

Scipio Africanus was the son of a famous Roman general. He had survived the disaster at Cannae and actually enhanced his reputation by rebuilding the morale of that battle's survivors. In 211 BCE, Scipio's father fell in battle in Spain, and Scipio ascended to the generalship. Young and gifted, Scipio drove the Carthaginian army out of the Iberian Peninsula by surprising a garrison in 209 BCE and smashing an army led by Hannibal's brother.

In response, the Carthaginians came to Spain, but Scipio, in 206 BCE, expressed all of his military talent and strategic acumen in a victory at Ilipa. The Romans finally had a military figure to match Hannibal, and the Romans revered Scipio as a savior of the Republic. So great was his reputation that his plan for a direct assault on Carthage gained support.

Scipio Africanus saw a simple truth: if Hannibal was in Rome, then he wasn't in Carthage. This meant that Carthage lay open for attack. Scipio's army crossed the Mediterranean into Tunisia and besieged Carthage. Upon hearing the news, Hannibal left Rome to defend his home territory, and the two titans of military strategy clashed at Zama in 203 BCE (sixteen years after the famous crossing of the Alps).

The Roman army consisted of war-hardened veterans and had the leadership of a proven general. Hannibal led soldiers mostly new to war into battle. The ensuing Roman victory brought an end to Hannibal's campaigns, and the Carthaginians agreed to decidedly unequal peace terms. Despite the theatrics of the crossing of the Alps and Hannibal's early victories, Rome proved superior to the Carthaginians and would rule the Mediterranean.

Deprived of his armies and abandoned by the Carthaginian elite, Hannibal spent the rest of his life dodging Roman vengeance. He fought his old enemy one last time in 190 BCE and again lost. Eight years later, the Romans caught up with Hannibal as he sought refuge at the court of an obscure king. About to be handed over, Hannibal instead killed himself.

## Dot 13: One More Time

By 199 BCE, one of the Republic's vainest politicians, known as Cato the Elder, rose to prominence despite having been born outside of Rome. Fear of Carthage continued to permeate much of Roman society. As an old man, Cato visited Carthage on a diplomatic mission and saw that Carthage had returned to her former glory. This large and powerful state could vie again for power in the Mediterranean if she was not checked.

Upon returning to Rome, Cato immediately agitated for war and reminded the senators of how close Carthage stood to the Republic should war break out. Ever the showman and opportunist, Cato found his audiences receptive, and he ended every single speech he gave in the Senate, regardless of the topic, with the phrase *Delenda est Carthago*—or, to put it less poetically in English, *Carthage must be destroyed*.

And so it was, but not in Cato's time. In the year 147 BCE, the Carthaginians attacked the lands of one of Rome's allies, and the Roman Scipio Aemilianus took the opportunity to confront the old North African enemy. Laughably, the Roman Senate promised to forego an invasion if the Carthaginians would only pick up and move further away. The Cathaginians said no. Leading the charge, Scipio went into Carthage and persevered through the Carthaginian resistance. Rising on his popularity, Scipio soon found himself appointed consul.

In 146 BCE, Scipio and his men stormed into Carthage and sacked the city. Roman soldiers slaughtered the defenders in their houses, stole their possessions, and enslaved the survivors. Not content with all this blood, they then tore down every building and salted the land so no crops could ever again grow. Then they cursed the place against further settlement and left.

Scipio is remembered as the most significant Roman man of his era. He was the first man to shave every day. He never lost control of himself, and he had no qualms about slaughtering a whole civilization because of the theoretical threat they represented. He died in his sleep. Some people thought his wife had something to do with it, but history provides no definitive answer.

## Connecting the Dots

When the Romans conquered Syracuse during the Second Punic War, they snuffed out the mathematical tradition of the Greeks. Roman philosophy had no room for math and placed no emphasis on theory and abstraction. Rome's number system consisted of cumbersome Roman numerals, helpful for keeping track of military divisions but useless for anything else.

Rome's vast and long-lived civilization produced exactly zero mathematicians of note. Without a mathematical or theoretical background, Roman civilization proved to be incapable of synthesizing complex and abstract ideas. Mathematics, and with it the theoretical improvements that make technological progress more impressive, would not return to the Western world until the Renaissance.

The Roman intellect was instead interested in engineering and rhetoric. Engineering produced roads that connected the sprawling Republic and also underpinned the creation of monumental architecture, the kinds of awe-inspiring buildings that remind the bumpkins of who is in charge. Rhetoric, or argument, proved useful for senators who sought to outdo each other in verbal arenas.

But by the end of the Punic Wars, Rome's faults became more noticeable. Overreliance on the military produced powerful generals connected to their troops by a sense of personal loyalty. The government sometimes seemed to lack a core, shifting as it did depending upon the political circumstances. Perhaps, too, in their fear of the outside world, the Romans had gone too far. By butchering the Carthaginians and salting the earth of Carthage, the Romans revealed an inability to restrain the fear and hatred that would eventually consume the Republic.

**CHAPTER EIGHT**
# THE HAN

## Dot 1: Connections and Sources

With Carthage no longer in existence, the Punic Wars ended. By this time, a powerful new dynasty paralleled Rome in China. With the death of Qin Shi Huangdi, China seemed set to again dissolve into a fragmented state similar to that of India. Instead, it produced over four centuries of impressive cultural and intellectual achievements.

The Han Dynasty, in various incarnations, lasted from 206 BCE to 220 CE. This means that at the time of the second Punic War, when Scipio began to seriously threaten Hannibal, the Han Dynasty had entered its formative phase. While all of the high drama of Caesar's triumph over the Republic was occurring, the Han Dynasty flourished. By the time of the Han collapse in 220 CE, Rome had long since abandoned her republican roots and for well over two centuries had become a politically unstable empire.

In the early fourth century, under Constantine, Rome's history intersected with that of early Christianity in a historically significant way. While the Roman government embraced and shaped Christianity, China had already sunk into a fractured period of medieval-style politics.

## Dot 2: The Han

Much of what historians know about Han China comes from the pen of Sima Qian, the son of a minor nobleman who started his writing career as a free-living poet during the reign of Emperor Wu Di. The unfortunate

## CHAPTER EIGHT

man seems to have enjoyed tweaking people in power, and when he stood up for a defeated general who had surrendered in battle, the royal family had him arrested. The imperial family gave Sima a choice: pay an enormous fine or suffer castration. Sima did not have the money, so, well, *snip snip*. Usually castrati, faced with such public humiliation, chose to commit suicide, but Sima opted to live and write history. His massive work lives on as a primary source for Chinese historians.

When Qin Shi Huangdi died, power passed to his son Hu-Hai, who had just entered his twenties. The young ruler borrowed his father's cruel techniques but lacked the mystique his predecessor had earned over years of military conquest. Hu-Hai acted out on his paranoia about revolution by ordering the execution of anyone he thought might have plans to threaten his power. In one grotesque example of his legalistic governing philosophy, Hu-Hai ordered the drawing and quartering of ten women. ("Drawing and quartering" sounds like a mathematical term, but it refers to a vicious form of execution where a person's four limbs are tied to four separate horses and then ripped from the body.)

Having thus sowed fear in the Chinese population, Hu-Hai found himself more afraid of the people than ever and encircled his palace with thousands of soldiers. Hiding is rarely the best strategy for an emperor, and within a few months a rebellion broke out in China's southern region. The people of the old kingdoms, who had not lost their political identity during the brutal reign of the Qin, asserted their political independence, and it looked as if chaos would again consume China's politics. Hu-Hai descended into a rage-fueled madness that led some of his associates to plan a coup. Faced with seizure and execution, he chose suicide.

## Dot 3: Three Kingdoms

For a little more than a month, Hu-Hai's distant cousin ruled, but then a general from the rebellious Chu province stormed into the palace along with his allies and instituted a massacre of everything Qin. The rebels slaughtered everyone, stole the treasure, and set the palace on fire. The Qin Dynasty had been built upon terror and was incinerated by rage. The successful rebels carved the former dynasty into three provinces, or kingdoms, thus instituting the Three Kingdoms Era.

Five years of political disunion followed after the massacre of the Qin until one of the warlords, Liu Pang, asserted his dominance over the others. An unlikely leader, Liu came from a family of peasants but had been selected for a government post. During the uprising, Liu allied with the right people and gained a fiefdom, which he called Han, as a reward. When political assassinations sparked a power struggle among the three kingdoms, Liu marched on the other rulers. By 202 BCE, Liu and his associates cornered the initial rebel leader, Hsiang Yu, who chose suicide over capture or execution.

Having reunited China, Liu Pang changed his name to Gao Zu (he is sometimes referred to as Gaodi) and chose the name of his initial power base, the Han, for his dynasty. Even as emperor, Gao Zu never let go of his peasant origins. He once demonstrated his feelings for the court scholars by relieving his bladder in one of their hats.

He also used his peasant roots to appeal to the largely agrarian Chinese people, instituting a series of welcome changes. Tradition took a central place in Han philosophy, and Gao Zu abandoned the vicious legalistic philosophy of the Qin. Instead, Gao Zu hoped to govern China by assigning his sons and close associates to regions around China.

## Dot 4: The Barbarians

During this time, empires of substantial size risked being picked apart at the fringes by horse-riding nomads. The most feared nomads of the era are now known as the Huns, and the riches of China attracted these barbarians to the northern border. Gao Zu himself was nearly killed in one battle against the Huns in 201 BCE, a trauma that seems to have made him realize the futility of finding a military solution to the problem. Instead, Gao Zu decided to make alliances with the Hun chiefs by arranging marriages with women from the Han royal family. Hun chiefs could expect lavish wedding gifts in addition to a bride, something that kept them from staging raids.

Military clashes broke out on occasion anyway, and in 195 BCE Gao Zu decided to attend one of these battles. A random arrow took him out. During his reign, Gao Zu took many wives and had several children. His direct instruction had been to pass power on to his first son from his second wife, but once dead he had no way to enforce his wish, and a power struggle seized the court.

## Dot 5: Court Intrigue

Gao Zu's first wife, Lu, did not like his choice for succession. She poisoned the presumptive heir and had his mother (Gao Zu's second wife) blinded and cut up for pig food. When her son, Huidi, became emperor at the age of fifteen, he had already learned not to mess with his mom. Huidi died young, and Empress Lu governed as dowager while a series of infants and children, all related to the royal family, technically sat on the throne. Lu's viciousness, at least according to the disaffected court members who wrote her history, seems to have extended deep into China, but, for all of this, power again reverted to the local warlords.

Empress Lu's death in 180 BCE caused rebellions among the more powerful warlords previously subordinated to her. In the power struggle, everyone seems to have developed momophobia, or fear of moms (okay, this is a made-up word, but it fits well here), specifically the mothers of young rulers. Few people wanted a return to the days when weak-willed children did the bidding of a powerful and nefarious mother. One of the rulers of a sub-kingdom instead ascended the throne and took the title of Wendi.

## Dot 6: Wendi and Jingdi—The Golden Age

Despite the attention the tyrants receive, Chinese history contains more than one long-serving and benevolent ruler. The first of these was Wendi, who ruled from 180 to 157 BCE. Reforms mark his reign, from lessening the brutality of the legal code to protection from natural disasters to competent management of state assets. Confucianism's place in Chinese society deepened, and scholars were elevated in status. Just as important, Wendi left the Han Dynasty with a clear plan of succession.

Now here's where things get strange again: Wendi's son Jingdi, who assumed the throne in 157 BCE, would be haunted by a childhood horror. As an eight-year-old, Jingdi and another little boy from one of the subordinate royal families (the house of Wu) got into an argument. Jingdi picked up a board and struck his playmate with it until the boy died. Apparently, the incident engendered a deep need for revenge in the boy's father. When Jingdi assumed the throne, the king of Wu raised a rebellion along with some of his allies. The emperor's military put the rebellion down, an act that solidified Han rule over the occasionally rebellious outlands.

In Han histories, the reigns of Wendi and Jingdi are treated as a golden age. The long-serving emperors established firm control of the fractious kingdoms and alleviated the burden of legalistic laws on the peasantry. Perhaps most important, the ideology of Confucianism found a home at the royal court.

## Dot 7: Wudi and the Military

Upon the death of Jingdi in 141 BCE, Wudi became emperor. Wudi, who would reign all the way up until 87 BCE (at fifty-four years, his reign ranks with the longest of any ruler in history), towers over the classical period of the Han. Only fifteen at the time of his ascension, Wudi quickly established his power over "advisers" in his family who wished to rule as regents, as Empress Lu had done. So impressive and innovative was China during the reign of Wudi that the achievements from that period of China's history can be understood by studying his life.

During Wudi's reign, Chinese court philosophers developed the notion that China possessed a superior form of civilization. This concept lent moral power to the idea that the Chinese could invade the barbarian groups as a way of establishing peace. Wudi never rode with his troops, but Chinese armies spread into the north and the south, driving the barbarians, mostly a tribe known as the Xiongnu, away from the Han political core.

Along the way, Chinese armies overran both Vietnam and Korea. The Chinese military marched so far to the west that they fought in central Asia. At one point, Chinese soldiers faced off against a few Roman soldiers who had been captured and forced to serve their Greek masters at a kingdom called Sogdiana. The Chinese, two thousand miles away from the Han capital, won this bizarre battle.

In fact, the Chinese expansionist impulse led Wudi to dispatch a traveler named Zhang Qian to the West, where he visited the regions of Parthia (these were the first people to be able to shoot backward while riding on a horse—a kind of deadly circus trick—and the maneuver still bears the name of "Parthian shot"). Qian returned in 126 BCE full of stories. Eventually, the greatest of Parthian kings, Mithridates II, would send envoys to Han China, thus establishing contact between two of the great empires of the ancient East.

## Dot 8: Silk Road

As is often the case, military expansion connected the dots of two of the most important early civilizations: China and Parthia. As is also often the case, residents of the two regions quickly took a liking to the new and foreign goods they encountered from their new trade contacts. As a result, lines of trade were spun between the two civilizations, and these lines were made of silk.

In time, the famous Silk Road would link China with Europe. Few people, if any, ever traveled the entire length of the road, but goods could pass like a baton between traders and eventually arrive at the distant ends. Of course, the expense of traveling all that way meant that when the silk did arrive in the West, the cost had grown prohibitive to most buyers, which only seemed to have made the item more desirable for wealthy Westerners.

Surely, nobody to the west could have imagined that the fine material was derived from something so wriggly and unattractive as a worm, but then they would have had no way of knowing. The Chinese government kept a close watch on the secret and punished with death anyone who revealed how to make silk.

## Dot 9: Civil Service Exams

By the time of Wudi, Chinese power had been firmly consolidated under the Han emperor, but reform proved necessary. The administration brought back a formalized tax code and, just as important, took over the trade in salt. Controlling the massive salt trade kept money flowing into the Han treasury. Yet, by Wudi's time, corruption had infested the rank of civil servants. Wudi wanted a competent bureaucracy and needed to find a way ensure that his advisers and officials could do their jobs.

Toward this end, the Chinese instituted a program of educating and testing. The latter became known as the civil service exam, an innocuous term that does not capture the intellectually brutal process of study required to pass the test. In short, Chinese students who aspired to be in the civil service would begin studying during childhood, usually under the tutelage of someone who had not passed the exam and had to become a teacher. After years of immersion in the philosophy of Confucianism, wannabe bureaucrats would sit in a cubicle and write for days on end. Then the answers would be taken from them (and sometimes rewritten so that the handwriting could not identify the candidate). With all identifying markers removed from the work, a collection of elite scholars graded the essays.

In this way, the Chinese ensured that people involved in government had undergone a rigorous education. The exam process highlights a fundamental difference between the Chinese and the Greeks and the Romans. The Chinese did not view government as a democratic process, where officials should answer to the people (or at least some of the people); instead, they viewed government officials in much the way that modern people view professionals. Nobody wants a dentist who has been voted into the position; you want someone who has been trained, tested, and licensed. Doctors, lawyers, and teachers all must go through such a process. The Chinese merely extended the same logic to government officials.

Men who passed the exams entered an elite world. To be a Chinese civil servant meant to be a cultivated gentleman, equally adept in the arts and in statecraft. Many servants would grow long fingernails as a sign of status; this demonstrated that they did not have to engage in the manual labor that defined the lives of the peasantry. To fill their free time, most servants painted landscapes coupled with poems. The Romans, meanwhile, seemed to have less cultivated tastes, preferring to watch the gore pile up in the Coliseum.

## Dot 10: Wudi's End

By the end of his reign, Wudi seems to have lost some sense of proportion. The economic changes instituted when he claimed the Mandate of Heaven proved effective in strengthening the economy. However, by the end of his reign the land taxes had been lowered so much on the nobility to keep their favor that taxes on salt had to rise.

Salt is so ubiquitous in the modern world that it may be hard to imagine a time when it was scarce. Yet history and medical science indicate that a lack of salt in the diet produces serious negative effects. Also, in the years before refrigeration, salt played a crucial role in curing meat so that it would last. This is why the act of raising taxes on salt, along with a good many important metals, led to rising peasant anger toward the crown.

For all his political acumen, Wudi believed deeply in the supernatural and the superstitious. Old, enfeebled, and surrounded by meddling concubines and peasant discontent, the emperor called in a series of sorcerers to protect him from witches. Of course, he also searched for some banal secret to immortality (a conceit so common among ancient emperors as to elicit boredom). When his best general surrendered to the barbarians and Sima Qian defended him, Wudi had him castrated. Sima found a solace of sorts, it appears, in writing the history of China.

Eventually it was not witches but ordinary women who drove Wudi out. A rebel family, the Li, targeted his favorite concubine. Wudi raised her status but found no support when the Li stormed the capital. The old man hid in the countryside, and his mistress hanged herself. Not long after that the Han's greatest emperor died.

## Dot 11: From Wudi to Wang Mang

Between 87 BCE and 49 BCE, a succession of minor rulers claimed the Mandate of Heaven, some for only a few days, and some whose youth made them susceptible to the intents of their advisers. Wudi's grand schemes reformed China and etched Wudi's reign into history, but they also proved to be expensive. Excessive spending depleted the treasury while excessive taxation caused rebellion. None of the successors of Wudi possessed either the personality or the mystique necessary to reintroduce the salt or iron taxes to a potentially rebellious peasant population.

In 33 BCE, a man named Chengdi assumed the Mandate of Heaven, but he proved ill suited to reforming China. Instead of governing, he watched cockfights and busied himself with his harem. Then Heaven revoked his mandate; the Yellow River flooded and drowned several villages. Chengdi tried to blame one of his chief advisers and had the man executed as a scapegoat. But Chengdi's wife had a nephew, known as Wang Mang, who seized control of the moment.

Mang organized several hundred boats and rescued victims of the flood. He then organized labor to construct bulwarks and dig diversionary trenches. Chengdi, meanwhile, proved incapable not only of rescuing his subjects but also of having a male heir. When the emperor died in 7 BCE, three rulers took the throne for a short series of reigns that saw rising taxes and an end to the occupation of most of Korea. Eventually, Wang Mang finagled a child onto the throne while he ruled as a regent.

With the Han weakened, rumors of Wang's supernatural background, perhaps even his connection to China's myths, made him seem like a man of imperial destiny. He had saved China from the anger of the Yellow River and put down revolts against his throne. In 9 CE, he dissolved the Han Dynasty and declared the arrival of the Xin Dynasty. Roughly translated, Xin means "new," but it might as well have meant "short," as it lasted only fourteen years, until 23 CE.

Wang rebuilt things, bringing back respect for the Confucian scholars and taxation of the major commodities in the process. But many still considered him a usurper, someone who had no blood tie to the imperial family. Discontent continued under the surface, and then the Yellow River, which had given Mang the opportunity to rise in prominence, flooded again. The Yellow River giveth, and it taketh away. A rebel group whose members painted their foreheads red, and were known therefore as the Red Eyebrows, challenged Mang's rule. The Red Eyebrows overwhelmed the imperial army.

A member of the Han lineage, seeing his chance to reestablish the Han, restructured the empire. The Red Eyebrows stormed into the capital, hunting Mang. After several days of brutal street-to-street fighting, the rebels burned down the capital and captured Mang. They separated his head from his body, a sure sign that he'd lost the Mandate of Heaven.

## Connecting the Dots

The Han Dynasty's early period corresponded roughly with the decline of the Roman Republic to the west. Julius Caesar's life paralleled the chaotic period following the death of Wudi, and Augustus Caesar, the first true emperor of Rome, was a contemporary of Wang Mang. This narrative will eventually come back to the second period of the Han Dynasty. For now, it's time to return Rome, where the balance between freedom and fear began to tip toward the latter, and where democracy would devolve into empire.

## CHAPTER NINE
# FROM REPUBLIC TO EMPIRE IN ROME

### Dot 1: The Deaths of the Gracchus Brothers

Rome's destruction of Carthage may also have proved to be the destruction of the Republic itself. Many of the senators decried that the Republic's best days had ended with the dismantling of their old North African enemy. A new foe, the Numidians, emerged from deeper within Africa. At this time, Gaius Marius, a man from a plebeian background, gained fame through his military exploits. He had the Numidian leader plucked from his African homeland, shackled, and displayed like a trophy. Marius's reward came in the form of five elections to become consul. That this was unconstitutional hardly mattered, as Marius's military fame seemed to justify such extralegal activity. Yet it eroded the very respect for the law upon which the entire system was based. Marius created a precedent that Julius Caesar would take full advantage of later.

After they destroyed it, the Romans renamed Carthage "Africa," which meant "sunny place." With Carthage gone, Rome's major problem lay in trying to assimilate thousands of new slaves taken from the conquered regions. Roman law contained no middle ground: slaves had no legal rights at all, but if a slave master freed a slave, that person became an immediate citizen. The new slaves eventually revolted in the First Servile War in the year 135 BCE, but, like all slave revolts in history (save one), it failed.

Still, the revolt took three years to quell, and clearly Rome had a social problem. The wealthy landowners took much of the newly conquered

## CHAPTER NINE

land and filled it with slaves. The Romans were smart enough to not train their slaves to fight, so only freemen could be drafted into the military. In practice, this meant that only peasants had to fight in the wars, and then usually either to protect the landholdings of the wealthy or to add to them.

One of the tribunes, a relatively young man named Tiberius Gracchus, set out to change this policy. The law reforms he proposed, however, got shot down by the other tribunes who were part of the upper classes. Tiberius used his political power to get his bill put up for a vote, and along the way he became a hero to the plebeian masses. In 132 BCE, while gossip and rumor infected the senatorial chambers, Tiberius put himself up for reelection as tribune. Most people felt that the other tribunes or the senators would either kill Tiberius or prevent his election.

Maybe he had a headache or maybe he had a plan, but Tiberius put his palm on his head, and many saw this as a sign to fight. The crowd in the chambers revolted, and one of the tribunes bludgeoned Tiberius with a stool leg. He and a few hundred rebels died, and their murderers tossed the bodies into the Tiber River.

With these acts, violence entered the Senate, pushing out debate and the rule of law. It would do so again eight years later when Tiberius's younger brother, Gaius, ran for the tribune position and won. When he tried to revive his brother's reforms and enact laws to improve the lives of the poor, he was opposed by the consuls. Gaius raised a small army against the consuls; when fighting broke out between the two factions, he, too, was killed.

The victors removed the head from Gaius's corpse and put it on display. His body, along with the corpses of about three thousand other rebels, joined his brother's in the Tiber. Those in power were reluctant to give it up, and only someone with superior military strength could control the Senate and consuls. But someone like that, the Romans would find, was not likely to stop using violence once in power.

## Dot 2: The Social War

The concept of assimilation underpinned the social network of Rome. The disparate people of the empire could aspire to citizenship, which dampened the type of discontent that can smolder into rebellion. In about 170 BCE, Rome dispensed with the process of assimilation and stopped accepting outer groups as citizens. Many warned of the dangers of this policy but were not heeded.

In 91 BCE, some anonymous Italians stabbed a Roman official named Livius Drusus in the groin and he died. This triggered a large-scale rebellion, most of which occurred between 90 and 89 BCE, which surprised the out-of-touch Senate. Though old and out of shape, Marius came out of retirement (he'd left the consulship before his sixth election) but found that most of his troops preferred a younger and more energetic general named Sulla.

Sulla's armies defeated the rebels to the south, something that elevated his already powerful reputation in the eyes of his fellow Romans. By 88 BCE, his actions (plus the savvy policy of the Senate, which awarded citizenship to the regions that did not rebel) had brought an end to the rebellion. Despite his fame, Sulla was not awarded a consulship, but he was consoled by being given another important military assignment to the east.

## Dot 3: Sulla's Return

Despite being old, overweight, and in bad health, Marius wanted the military appointment that his rival Sulla had gotten. He was clearly the wrong man for the job but bought his way into it anyway. The tribune he bribed, named Sulpicius, raised a private army and forced the Senate to give the appointment to Marius. When a couple of tribunes went to Sulla's army to announce the change of leadership, the soldiers murdered them with thrown stones.

Sulla himself appeared reluctant to give up his post just because of the jealousy of an old man and his corrupt bargain with a tribune. Back in Rome, Marius instituted a slaughter of those close to Sulla. The senators begged Sulla to turn his army over, but, in a move predating Caesar's crossing of the Rubicon, Sulla gathered his army and headed toward Rome.

The Roman Constitution forbade any consul from asserting military power within the city walls. This was considered the Senate's property. Sulla disregarded this rule and ordered his men into the interior, and then he told them to burn the homes of his rivals. Sulla himself carried a torch.

Marius ran away to North Africa, and Sulla ordered the Senate to convene and issue punishments to his enemies. They did. He ordered

CHAPTER NINE

a new election; they elected someone other than Sulla—a man named Cinna. Sulla promised his allegiance and then headed back to his war. The Roman Constitution had once again been trampled on.

When Sulla left, the Senate tossed Cinna out. Marius, by now, had gone crazy during his exile. His bodyguards murdered anyone he accused of disloyalty, and he made a lot of accusations. Sulla, meanwhile, conquered Asia Minor and brought the Greek states back under Roman control. Then he turned back toward Rome. Marius, hearing about this, bravely drank himself to death.

Cinna proved a little braver and raised an army to fight Sulla. His army, however, did not share his positive outlook and chose to murder him rather than fight. The Roman citizens, seeing the disarray and corruption of the Senate and its affiliates, favored Sulla more and more. Finally, Marius's son led an army in an attempt to head Sulla off, but they were vanquished, and in 83 BCE Sulla again marched his armies into Rome. (Two youthful commanders, Crassus and Pompey, accompanied him. In time they would play a greater part in the demise of the Republic.)

Anyone who had fought against Sulla (roughly six thousand people, according to Plutarch) was taken prisoner. Sulla filled the Roman Circus with these men and gave a speech to the Senate. He had to speak loudly, lest the screams of the prisoners drown out his words; he had them all slaughtered while he calmly delivered his address. It is doubtful that many remembered his words, but he got his point across.

In 81 BCE, the Senate made Sulla a dictator. The constitution allowed for this only in a crisis situation, but at the time Rome was under no threat save for that which Sulla represented. Once in power, Sulla and his henchmen, Pompey and Crassus, set about stealing property and purging Rome of Sulla's enemies. In 80 BCE, having butchered his opponents and the Roman Constitution, Sulla retired. Then, for whatever reason, his bowels corroded and burst open, and in 78 BCE he died. The Republic would live on, but only briefly.

## Dot 4: Spartacus

Romans liked spectacle, and they liked it bloody. While a variety of brutal entertainments took place in the Roman arenas, history and popular culture best remember the gladiatorial battles, which likely began in the year 264 BCE. Technically, gladiators were slaves, but, as the best-known athletes of the day (many were captured from the wars of conquest the Romans regularly engaged in), they also appear to have been lionized by their fans.

By 73 BCE, five years after the death of Sulla, Plutarch writes that seventy-eight gladiators escaped their confinement and armed themselves with tools from a butcher shop. They then used their weapons to butcher a small contingent of Roman soldiers. The leader who emerged went by the name of Spartacus. He was technically a barbarian but had a reputation for intelligence.

When the authorities heard of the rebellion, they dispatched three thousand Roman soldiers. Soon enough, the gladiator army found itself trapped up a mountain, but they hacked away at vines in the forest to make ladders. They escaped down a cliff and surprised and slaughtered a Roman encampment. Clever. Several victories against Roman legions followed, and a historian named Appian claimed that Spartacus at one time led up to seventy thousand men.

Spartacus's only intent seems to have been to return to his Thracian homeland, but his followers got cocky and wanted to crush Rome itself. The Romans raised a large army this time, eventually sending the consuls to lead it. The gladiators defeated this army. Crassus was then sent, and his army fought but then ran away. Enraged, Crassus had his troops decimated (every randomly chosen tenth man killed).

Spartacus hoped to get his army to Sicily, but the pirates of the Mediterranean with whom he made a deal ripped him off. The men in his army had by now lost respect for the Roman military might. Regardless of orders to the contrary, they charged Crassus's front lines. Demoralized the soldiers may have been, but these were still members of the Roman legions. The Roman forces drove back the gladiators, and someone killed Spartacus during the retreat.

Pompey had no interest in letting Crassus get the glory, so he sped to the battle site and rounded up most of the retreating gladiators. He then decorated the roads to Rome with the crucified corpses of the slave rebels. Pompey took credit for the victory, and in 70 CE both he and Crassus managed to get elected to the position of consul.

CHAPTER NINE

## Dot 5: Pompey

Pompey emerged as the senior partner in the consulship. Remember those pirates who swindled Spartacus? Well, there were a lot of them in the Mediterranean, and the Senate wanted them gone. Pompey led a large force to drive them out, and his success made him the best-known man in Rome and the clear successor to Crassus.

Enter Julius Caesar. The ambitious Caesar asked for the hand of Pompey's daughter (named Pompeia) in marriage and got an affirmative answer. (Just to increase the creepy factor, as a way of tying themselves together in an alliance, Pompey would later marry Caesar's daughter, despite being twenty-five years older than her.) By 66 BCE, Pompey conquered all the way to Jerusalem, where he established Roman control over the Jewish region of Palestine. He came home more beloved than ever.

## Dot 6: The Triumvirate

In 59 BCE, Caesar got himself elected to two important positions—one religious and one financial. But his mind, so brilliant in matters military and political, had no gift for finance. He ran up a debt that Crassus paid. Caesar then suggested that he and Crassus, along with Pompey, form a triumvirate (three-headed government). While the actual legal makeup of the Triumvirate remains murky, Caesar became a consul but acted on the behest of his new associates. As shady as the deal was, it proved popular. The one man who protested in the Senate got animal dung dumped on his noggin, which seemed to dampen any criticism.

## Dot 7: Enter Cicero

By 63 BCE, the great orator, writer, and statesman Cicero became an elected consul. Cicero possessed an intellectual gift and educated tongue, but no glorious family history. Despite the political intrigue of the time, and the way in which personality and politics between Caesar, Crassus, and Pompey dominated the end of the Republic, many historians nonetheless refer to the Republic's final years as "the age of Cicero."

Born in 106 BCE, Cicero's courage and intellect were made apparent in 81 BCE when he stood up to Sulla by defending a man's actions against one of Sulla's men. Later, when another of Sulla's protégés, named

Catiline, ran against Cicero for the consulship in 63 BCE, Cicero gave the man an eloquent verbal bludgeoning that has been recorded as the *Catilinarian Orations*. Catiline raised a rebellion and was killed, and Cicero ordered that the man's co-conspirators in Rome be executed. This proved that Cicero could do more than just speak well.

Cicero made friends with Julius Caesar, but he refused to always toady to the whims of the Triumvirate. Tired of being bullied into defending the associates of the Triumvirate in court, in 56 BCE he stood up to his masters by giving up politics. In exile, Cicero occupied his mind with philosophy. Politics, in time, would again recruit Cicero but only during the tumult of the Rome's civil war.

## Dot 8: Caesar in Gaul

Pompey still reigned as the senior partner in the Triumvirate. Recognizing this, Caesar went on a military campaign to the north in Gaul. Caesar later wrote about his military ventures in Gaul, including the brutality exhibited against the Frankish tribes. In the "Gallic Wars" Caesar penned his own history of conquest in the region. Unlike Alexander, Caesar did not typically fight on the front lines (although, in 57 BCE, caught in a surprise attack by the Nervii tribe, Caesar had to fight and did so successfully). Instead, he issued orders from just behind the lines and supposedly seized retreating soldiers by the throat and turned them back around to the battle.

In 52 BCE, a tribe called the Arverni, led by a man with the challenging name of Vercingétorix, drove back a group of Roman soldiers who were in the process of attempting a siege. Caesar learned from this. Vercingétorix staged a series of small attacks on the retreating Roman army but eventually had to retreat to a hilltop. Instead of attacking from the front again, Caesar ordered a siege set up.

But Vercingétorix had yet to play his whole hand. He had allies in the region, and the Romans had strayed far from home. Gallic relief forces arrived, but Caesar was prepared. Between September 28 and October 3, the Romans and the Gallic tribes battled in brutal front-line fighting, with Caesar riding up and the down the lines.

On October 2, Caesar himself, attired in a scarlet cloak, led the counterattack. The Roman soldiers first splintered and then broke the relief

CHAPTER NINE

army sent to relieve Vercingétorix's people. The Romans subsequently drove the survivors of the battle away.

On October 3, Vercingétorix, seeing his situation clearly, rode to Caesar's camp and surrendered. Caesar treated the man like a war trophy, sending him back to Rome to be displayed in chains. Then, in 46 BCE, when the novelty wore off, Caesar ordered his old enemy to be strangled to death. In Gaul, Caesar demonstrated the power of his mind and the competence of his rule. That he lacked empathy for his rivals hardly would have counted against him in that era.

## Dot 9: The Rubicon

Caesar fought in Gaul to enhance his glory and amass military power. The eloquence of Caesar's historical account of his battles in Gaul masks the nearly genocidal brutality with which the Romans invaded and butchered the Gauls. Many in the Roman Senate viewed Caesar as a power-hungry warmonger and recognized him as a danger to the principles of the Republic. Caesar, for a long while, seemed content to rule and fight in Gaul rather than return home to the messy politics of Rome.

Then Crassus, the most inconsequential member of the Triumvirate, died in 53 BCE, just one year after Caesar's daughter (the one married to Pompey) perished while giving birth, thus severing Caesar's crucial familial link with Pompey. Caesar had remained too long in Gaul; his absence had eroded his political strength at home. Many of the senators talked openly of prosecuting Caesar, maybe even of handing him over to his Gaulish enemies for ghoulish treatment.

In 48 BCE Caesar requested that he again be allowed to stand for the consulate. The Senate said no. Caesar's henchman, Marc Antony, attempted to bully the Senate but found that his enemies had teeth and was instead himself driven from Rome. The senators, looking to assert their power over their wayward general to the north, ordered that Caesar disband his army and return home. They had the backing of Pompey, who had long been considered the senior member of the Triumvirate.

In 49 BCE, Caesar, incensed at this blow to his prestige and confident that years of battle and plunder in Gaul had forged an unbreakable bond with his soldiers, turned his army southward. Eventually, they came to the Rubicon River, the natural boundary between Rome and Gaul. Crossing the Rubicon meant invading Rome and committing treason, but Caesar barely hesitated.

Plutarch has him shouting "*Alea iacta est!*" ("The die is cast!") before crossing the Rubicon. Caesar had indeed come home.

## Dot 10: Pompey's Death

At this point, Pompey must have realized the extent of his dilemma. Julius Caesar, a general who'd made his reputation as an eloquent butcher of men in the north, now marched at the head of Rome's most battle-tested and powerful armies. Pompey could raise but a few divisions to hurl at this conquering force. However, Pompey's soldiers saw what he did not—that fighting this army amounted to suicide. They refused, and Pompey ran to Greece.

Caesar stormed to Rome's treasury. One of the tribunes stepped in front of him to prevent the plunder. An amused Caesar brushed him aside with a remark to the effect of "I dislike giving the order to have you killed more than I dislike having it done." Well, then. The tribune wisely left Caesar to his riches.

Caesar followed Pompey, but his troops nearly starved in the pursuit. By 48 BCE Pompey had recovered and raised a large army of allies, but his military acumen had grown soft during all those years in Rome. Despite having much larger numbers of men, Pompey's army fell to Caesar's disciplined troops at the Pharsalus.

In the aftermath of the battle, Caesar showed his political genius. He held his men back from any post-victory slaughter of Pompey's troops. The vanquished were Roman citizens, not barbarian Gauls. Caesar did not intend to govern an empire of corpses, and he knew that he would need the support of the Romans in order to rule.

Pompey ran to Egypt, which was still ruled by the heirs of the Ptolemaic Dynasty, and Caesar followed. As it happened, Egypt's king, Ptolemy XIII, had no desire to see Pompey.

## Dot 11: Civil War

The youthful Ptolemy XIII ruled Egypt (although his sister, Cleopatra, then a teenager, coveted the throne). Ptolemy's tutor, Theodocius, saw the

CHAPTER NINE

inherent danger that came with harboring an enemy of Julius Caesar and suggested a simple solution. The Egyptians greeted Pompey as he arrived on his boat; then one of Ptolemy's soldiers thrust a sword through his back and severed his head.

Caesar soon arrived, and Ptolemy greeted the great conqueror with a present: Pompey's head. Caesar wept over his old friend, but even through watery eyes he could recognize the beauty of Cleopatra. He ordered both Ptolemy and Cleopatra to Alexandria. Caesar's soldiers killed Ptolemy when he resisted. Caesar left Egypt with Cleopatra in charge, and he left Cleopatra with his child in her womb.

Back in Rome, the people rolled out into the street in order to greet Caesar. The conqueror himself assumed the role of dictator and began giving orders and appointing people to offices. Time itself was made to bend to Caesar's will, as he created a new calendar, one that included a leap year, but Caesar's arrogance alienated the senators.

The senators feared Caesar, which was probably why, in 44 BCE, they both appointed him a dictator and killed him. At this point, Caesar, newly appointed as dictator for as long as he lived, had let his megalomania get the best of him. The word "dictator" did not suffice; he wanted to be a king.

His henchman, Marc Antony, tried to crown him with a laurel wreath during a religious celebration, but the crowd did not approve. The Senate appointed him as king despite Caesar's protestations. (Caesar's refusal of the crown was likely no more sincere than the tears he had shed over Pompey.) He could wear the crown outside of Rome, while on a military campaign against Parthia, but not in his home country.

Now all but an emperor, Caesar concerned himself with his lineage. At this time, Cleopatra had given birth to his child, but Caesar chose his articulate nephew, Octavian, as his heir. Just eighteen, Octavian had caught his uncle's attention a few years before by delivering an impressive funereal speech.

For the seething senators, such acts guaranteed the perpetual destruction of their Republic and their prestige. It was too much.

## Dot 12: The Ides of March

Brutus, a senator and Caesar's cousin, conspired with some of the other senators to kill Caesar and save the Republic. Their plan was to assassinate the newly appointed dictator on March 15—the so-called Ides of March. Plutarch writes that the senators assumed Marc Antony would stay loyal to Caesar, and so they plotted to distract him while they completed their bloody work on the Senate floor.

Caesar entered the Senate chamber. Tillius Cimber, whose brother had been exiled by Caesar, pretended to have a question but seized the robes of Caesar's toga, thus immobilizing him. Piqued at this treatment, the dictator tried to rise, but by then the senators had unveiled their knives.

The first assassin stabbed with such nervous intensity that he missed the vital organs; the knife penetrated Caesar's flesh above the collar bone. An orgy of knifing followed, with each senator taking a turn at drawing blood. In the killing frenzy, someone accidentally stabbed Brutus in the hand. Caesar, punctured thirty-five times, perished in a mass of bloody robes and torn flesh.

Plutarch tells us that Caesar, betrayed, uttered one shocked question during the assassination. "Even you, my son?" he asked Brutus. Shakespeare, taking poetic license, changed this to the more famous "*Et tu, Brute?*" in his classic play about Caesar.

## Dot 13: Great Caesar's Ghost

Even in dictatorships, power resides with popular opinion. No one knew how the Roman people would react to the assassination of Caesar. The senators may have fancied themselves as protectors of the Republic, but the citizens of Rome saw things differently. Corruption had long ago seeped into the Senate, and many considered Caesar a hero.

Before Caesar's corpse turned cold, Marc Antony began plotting his rise to power. He burst into the Senate chambers after the murder and stopped the senators from disposing of Caesar's body in the river. Allowing Antony to preserve the body proved to be a major mistake, as the funeral of Caesar would provide Antony with an opportunity to sway the opinions of the Romans.

Within days, a funeral pyre had been erected around Caesar's corpse. Even in death, Caesar proved a shrewd politician. In his will he had decreed that his massive fortune be divvied up among the people of Rome. There's nothing like giving away a fortune to improve one's reputation in the eyes of the people receiving it. Marc Antony further enflamed

CHAPTER NINE

the populace by waving Caesar's shredded and bloody toga before the funeral crowd.

The crowd turned into a mob and tore through the streets, searching for the conspirators who'd killed Caesar. They tore one man apart, wrongly thinking him to be a senator. They found none of Caesar's actual killers, as the men had been smart enough to depart the city.

## Dot 14: The Second Triumvirate

Eighteen-year-old Octavian returned to Rome and found a friend in the famous orator Cicero. Marc Antony viewed Octavian as a rival, but one too strong to assassinate. Instead, Marc Antony, Octavian, and another man named Lepidus entered into an alliance known as the Second Triumvirate.

In order to cement the alliance between Octavian and Antony, Antony married Octavian's sister (predictably named Octavia), but marriage could not quench his infatuation with Cleopatra, Queen of the Nile. Antony carried on a gossip-inducing love affair with the queen, and soon Cleopatra carried his children. She gave birth to a little boy and girl—twins like Romulus and Remus. Also like Romulus and Remus, these twins were nurtured by a she-wolf.

Cicero, the great senator, foresaw the death of republicanism when he looked into the six-eyed monster of the Triumvirate. Octavian abandoned his friendship now that it became inopportune. Lepidus, Antony, and Octavian decided to kill three hundred potentially disloyal men.

Antony singled out Cicero to die first. Then he ordered that Cicero's head, which had spoken against him the Senate, and his right hand, which had been used to write so many eloquent condemnations of Antony's tyrannical intents, be severed and brought to him. When he collected the body parts, maniacal giggles escaped from Antony's mouth. Antony ordered the head and hand to be hammered up above the Forum, for all to see.

Like Caesar, Marc Antony loved Cleopatra. Also like Caesar, he seems to have hoped that he could gain power by enhancing his military reputation in distant lands. However, his attempts to conquer Parthia petered out, and in 34 BCE Antony retired to Egypt. Octavian, at this point, figured he could openly declare war on Antony, but he needed senatorial approval. He somehow got hold of Antony's will, and when he had it read before the Senate (in violation of Roman law), the contents shocked the politicians: Antony had left his fortune to his twins via Cleopatra and requested that his grave be dug in the Egyptian sands rather than the fertile soil of Rome. Such a lack of patriotism proved too much for the senators to tolerate. They gave their blessing to Octavian for war.

As both sides mobilized for war, Plutarch tells us of a series of macabre experiments that Cleopatra performed on her slaves. She fed them poisons and watched them die, trying to discover which of the poisons killed while causing the least amount of pain. Finally, after watching a few of her subjects die relatively peacefully from the venom of a snake known as the asp, she decided she had found her mode of suicide.

Inexplicably, Antony chose to fight a naval battle against Octavian rather than relying on his steely infantry. At the battle of Actium, in the northern section of Greece, Antony watched as Octavian's superior fleet demoralized and defeated his own navy. Once the battle turned in Octavian's favor, many of Antony's men switched sides. Antony and Cleopatra retreated to Egypt and waited out the winter. Come spring, Octavian sent an attack force, and Antony knew he'd lost Rome.

Plutarch writes that Antony ordered a servant to kill him. The servant pulled his sword but committed suicide with it instead. Antony pushed a sword into his own intestines, but instead of dying he lingered on, screaming for someone to kill him out of mercy. Instead, the bystanders left the room. When Cleopatra heard about her lover's bungled suicide, she sent someone to retrieve him.

Cleopatra's minions hefted the gory mess that was now Marc Antony to Cleopatra. She would not open the doors but instead had him hauled toward her window. The poor wretch soon hung suspended from ropes in the air as Cleopatra and her servants pulled him toward the window. Once inside, Cleopatra wept and covered herself with her lover's blood. Then Antony died. There are many stories as to how Cleopatra later committed suicide, but the most dramatic involves her teasing an asp to pierce her arm with its poison.

Octavian, now master of Rome, had Antony's oldest son executed, thus ending any opportunity for him to revolt. He took over Egypt, ending the Ptolemaic line of rulers that had existed since the time of Alexander the Great's death. No victory had been so complete since the Romans salted the earth of Carthage after the Third Punic War. No republic would grow again in Italy for more than a millennium.

CHAPTER NINE

## Connecting the Dots

Sulla not only trampled the Roman constitution by using military force and murder to intimidate the Senate but also introduced Pompey and Crassus into the political world of Rome. These two men, following in the path of Sulla, would be overthrown in due course by Caesar.

Several of the weaknesses of the Republic's structure by now had been revealed. To begin with, most Roman soldiers felt loyalty primarily to their commander, rather than the Senate. The senators, after all, blocked any attempts to reform the unequal societal structure of Rome, something the murder of both Gracchus brothers highlighted. Second, the Senate possessed a good deal of military strength as well, and it would use violence and murder to hold on to its privileges. Finally, such a situation ensured that only someone with superior power could force the Senate to "reform." Such a person might prove popular, but it was not clear who would hold such a dictator accountable to the people.

The stories of Caesar crossing the Rubicon and of the civil war between Antony and Octavian make up much of what is known as "classical history." These histories uphold much of the Western literary, political, and legal system and therefore deserve in-depth attention. However, to include such detail about every aspect of the empire would stray too far from the principles of a world history narrative, and so the empire's history and its sudden convergence with Christian history in the fourth century will be encapsulated here. Historians divide the major families of Roman empires into categories, sometimes based on family name and sometimes based on circumstances. Those divisions will be included in the narrative.

Sources: While much of the source material comes from Plutarch, the most famous classical work about the first emperors of Rome comes from Suetonius. This historian was born in 69 CE and wrote several books of biographies. The only one to survive was *The Twelve Caesars*, a gossipy set of biographies about the first dozen men to govern Rome after the collapse of the Republic. Suetonius's work is part history and part tabloid, including as it does every whispered rumor about each of the emperors in addition to the historically significant occurrences. It makes for interesting reading.

# CHAPTER TEN
# AFTER CAESAR

## Dot 1: Augustus

By 30 BCE, Octavian emerged from the civil wars as Rome's emperor. To solidify his status, the Senate declared him Augustus, meaning "revered." The Senate considered Octavian's elevation a temporary matter. Augustus had brought peace to Rome after a long period of strife, and he enjoyed popularity with the people. Augustus's peaceful rule (perhaps history's best example of a "benign dictatorship") destroyed the Roman Republic as much as Caesar's crossing of the Rubicon since it convinced most people that it was better to have an emperor than a corrupt republic.

Augustus possessed none of his Uncle Caesar's military acumen. In 9 CE, his general Quinctilius Varus suffered Rome's worst defeat since Cannae against the Germanic tribes at the battle of the Teutoburg Forest. So devastated were the military and Augustus that he supposedly wandered about the royal palace muttering, "Quinctilius Varus, give me back my legions!"

Teutoburg proved that Augustus was no Caesar on the military front, but he proved smarter than Julius in other ways. Augustus would not be stabbed to death by senators or other conspirators. He created a private army for his own protection, known as the Praetorian Guard. Some artistic historians refer to an Augustan age of the arts. The Roman poet Virgil wrote the *Aeneid*, a sort of Roman version of the *Iliad* with a hero who seemed awfully similar to Augustus. So impressive was the work that later the Renaissance genius Dante Alighieri would choose Virgil to guide him through the afterlife in his epic work, *The Divine Comedy*.

# CHAPTER TEN

Meanwhile, Augustus also concerned himself with creating a line of rulers to succeed him upon his death. He originally adopted his grandchildren from his daughter Julia. But in the years 2 and 1 BCE both of the grandkids (young men by this time), named Gaius and Lucius, died in separate incidents. At age sixty-five, Augustus found himself desperate to name an heir. He had one stepson, Tiberius, whom Augustus had not treated very well, having exiled Tiberius's wife and celebrating Gaius and Lucius in his stead. Tiberius had led some successful military expeditions but dealt with his frustrations by retiring to a life of philosophy on the island of Rhodes. After the deaths of his grandsons, Augustus recalled Tiberius to Rome and appointed him as heir.

Old age and sickness show no respect even for the Caesars. Augustus died of chronic diarrhea in 14 CE. Tiberius became Caesar, a word that by then had become synonymous with "emperor."

## Dot 2: Tiberius and the Julio-Claudian House

Already fifty-four years old, Tiberius assumed the role of Caesar but was met with a skeptical, if not hostile, reception from the senators. Some of the Roman legions in the German Rhine revolted. Tiberius did little as emperor other than appoint his nephew, named Germanicus, as his successor. The man died, so his son, Caligula, was appointed in his stead.

When his own son Drusus died, Tiberius tired of politics and retired to beautiful island of Capri to focus on his perversions. In his absence, power resorted to the Senate, but the leader of the Praetorian Guard, Sejanus, threatened to usurp power. Tiberius then discovered that Sejanus and Drusus's wife had been entangled in a love affair and had arranged for the death of Drusus.

Tiberius returned to Rome and worked out his grief by having Sejanus arrested and executed, and by having several hundred Romans arrested, tortured, and killed. Then he died and left a monster in control of Rome.

## Dot 3: Caligula

"Caligula" was the nickname for Gaius Caesar Germanicus and meant "little soldier's boots" or "bootikin." Tiberius, the twisted old man, had tutored Caligula in the means of debauchery. At a young age Caligula showed a predilection for watching humans undergo torture, and his predatory appetites mirrored those of his teacher. Tiberius seems to have considered his mentoring of Caligula to have been an act of vengeance on the Roman people. When Tiberius died in 37 CE, Caligula became emperor.

Although Caligula originally made a show of humility before the Senate (every senator voted to give him absolute power) and enjoyed the adulation of the crowds, his madness soon consumed both him and Rome. Caligula's name is now synonymous with psychopathy. Suetonius records him engaging in every form of human ethical sickness, from incest to feeding prisoners to wild animals. Minor offenses, such as failing to fully recognize the glory of Caligula's intellect, could result in someone being sawn in half or imprisoned until death in a small cage. Often, when he gave the order to execute someone, he also required the parents of the victim to attend.

After nearly four years of this behavior, a plot formed among the Praetorian Guard to assassinate Caligula. Suetonius recounts two versions of the murder, but both involve the assassins stabbing Caligula to death on the floor of the Senate, and then being killed themselves by loyal members of Caligula's Germanic bodyguards. Caligula was twenty-nine years old at the time of his death. The Praetorian Guard's actions set up the conditions by which those who possessed the weapons could decide who governed Rome.

## Dot 4: Claudius

Oddly enough, the Praetorian Guard chose the next emperor. Much to his own surprise, the choice was the supposedly feeble Claudius. The Senate later confirmed him as emperor. In contrast to his youthful predecessor, Claudius assumed the throne at the mature age of fifty. Suetonius presents Claudius as a sort of benign old uncle.

Claudius failed to instill fear in the Romans, and he often allowed himself to be dominated by his subordinates. He supposedly slobbered a lot and suffered from tics. His stomachaches sometimes made him want to kill himself. Like most Romans, he enjoyed watching the bloody combat of the gladiatorial shows.

During Claudius's reign, the Roman legions conquered southern Britain, making it a part of the empire. Several people tried to kill

CHAPTER TEN

Claudius on multiple occasions (avoiding assassination was practically part of the job description of being a Caesar), but somebody, probably his fourth wife (and niece) Agrippina, finally succeeded in 54 CE. Her son, Nero, had already been made emperor by the time the Roman public heard about the death of Claudius.

## Dot 5: Nero

Claudius had adopted Nero (a nickname) when he'd married Nero's mom. Nero also married Claudius's daughter Octavia, who was technically his stepsister. Nero really shouldn't have been emperor, as Claudius had a legitimate son named Britannicus, who should have been next in line. But Nero took the throne nonetheless in the year 54 CE. Though he was only seventeen, the Senate titled Nero "Father of the Country." The teenage Caesar behaved well enough at first, but when his mentors Burrus and Seneca died, Nero's depravities revealed themselves.

Nero ordered that Britannicus be erased and, along the way, also ordered the executions of his own wife and mother. He fancied himself a singer and actor and would enter competitions. The theater audience could not leave for any reason, and apparently one woman even gave birth during a performance since she was barred from exiting. He loved horse racing, became a reliable presence at the events, and even raced a ten-horse team himself. On one occasion he fell from the chariot and barely crossed the finish line. But no matter how abysmal the performance, Nero always won.

"Crazy" doesn't quite describe Nero. He would dress up in animal skins, cage himself, and then, upon being released, bite at naked people tied to poles for the occasion. And this is one of his lesser crimes. The Roman treasury became a piggy bank used to fund Nero's twisted fantasies and grandiose architectural schemes. Nero's depravity, so prevalent, actually becomes tedious to read about in Suetonius's book.

After fourteen years of Nero's reign, an African governor named Galba decided to usurp the throne and led a rebellion. Thirty-one-year-old Nero appears to have been shocked at how little support he could muster from the Romans or his own imperial guard. According to Suetonius, the Senate turned on him, and Nero heard that the senators intended to capture him and give him a punishment called the "ancient style."

Nero inquired as to what the "ancient style" of punishment would entail. When told that it meant he would be told to take off all his clothes, stick his head into a V made of wood, and then be beaten to death with bars, he decided to end his own life. After whining for a long time, Nero stabbed himself in the throat. This was apparently not very efficient, as he thrashed about in agony for a lengthy period of time. His bulging eyes apparently disturbed even the hardened Roman soldiers who'd come to arrest him.

## Dot 6: Galba, Otho, Vitellius

Like Julius, Galba made his reputation on a military campaign. He'd led the conquest of Britain, which had been initiated under Claudius. In 68 CE, his rebellion drove Nero to suicide, and Galba assumed power via military coup. Nero's messy demise ended the family rule of the Caesars. Though not a pervert (in fact, Galba seems to have deeply loved his wife, and he refused to marry again after her death), Galba lacked popularity because of the means by which he'd taken power and because he refused to honor any of the awards and contracts Nero had put in place.

Galba came to power by rebellion, and he lost power in the same way. Marcus Salvius Otho, a companion of Nero's, led a rebellion when it became clear that Galba would not select him as his successor. Soldiers murdered Galba by a pool and hacked off his head. Since Galba was seventy-two years old and bald, one of the murderers had to carry the grisly trophy in his cloak instead of by the hair. Someone cut off Galba's thumb, stuffed it in the mouth, and gave it to Otho, who had the head paraded around on a spear.

Otho ruled all of ninety-five days, until his army lost to yet another contender for the throne in a battle in northern Italy. With this win, Vitellius assumed the role of Caesar. Otho took a drink of water, got a good night's rest, then woke up and stabbed himself in the heart.

Can you guess what happened to Vitellius? He spent his brief time as Caesar eating at massive banquets and having his enemies tortured and killed. Then, in October of 69, the commander Vespasian defeated Vitellius's armies. Vitellius tried to hide, but Vespasian's troops found him and dragged him through the streets by a noose placed around his neck. People mocked him and threw feces at him; the soldiers gave him the old

CHAPTER TEN

torture of small cuts (this involved making painful little nicks over much of the body), killed him, and then stuck a hook in his body and dragged him through the Tiber River.

## Dot 7: Vespasian and the Flavian Dynasty

Vespasian's usurpation brought a new ruling family to Rome: the Flavians. Vespasian had long been involved in Roman politics, and he had gone with Nero to Greece. He'd commandeered the squashing of a Jewish revolt just a few years before. After defeating Vitellius, the Senate made him emperor in the city of Alexandria in the year 69. A year later, the new emperor arrived in a Rome on the verge of collapse due to the political chaos that had gripped the capital since the death of Augustus.

Unlike many of the previous Caesars, Vespasian showed an interest in actual governance. He ordered the city rebuilt, established a prudent fiscal policy that restored the treasury (Nero's grotesque reign had bankrupted the throne), and even laid off a sizeable percentage of the Roman legion. Under Vespasian's reign, architects and workers built the famous Coliseum.

Vespasian showed no appetite for cruelty, and Suetonius even writes of him weeping when the law dictated that criminals be executed. A good-natured man who liked money, Vespasian goes down in history as a good emperor. In the year 79, when he was nearly seventy and consumed by diarrhea, Vespasian's pride forced him to stand up so he might perish on his feet like an emperor should. He did.

## Dot 8: Titus

The oldest son of Vespasian, named Titus, succeeded his father. A military man, Titus served under Nero and put down the Jewish revolt of the year 70, famously destroying the Temple in Jerusalem in the bargain. Bad luck plagued Titus's short time in power. In 79, just a few months after he became Caesar, Mount Vesuvius blew up in one of ancient history's best-known disasters. Then, in 80, plague again visited Rome, followed by a fire.

Despite this, everyone seemed to like him. Suetonius believed that the death of Titus amounted to a Roman catastrophe. Some sickness killed him in the year 81, after he'd reigned for just over two years. At his death, he was only forty-one years old, and most of the Romans mourned him.

## Dot 9: Domitian

By the time Titus's younger brother, Domitian, assumed the throne, the Caesars were on a two-reign winning streak. No ruler had been brutally murdered since Vitellius. Domitian's reign included several military successes in Germany, but then he found out that (gasp!) a bunch of people wanted to kill him.

He responded with a paranoid purge of any potential enemies (including a lot of senators and a few consuls) that only worsened his reputation. His favorite mode of torture involved burning the genitalia of any potential revolutionary until the man confessed or ratted out his fellow revolutionaries. This all caused more people to plot against his life.

In the year 96, after fifteen years as Caesar, an attendant named Stephanus agreed to assassinate Domitian. Stephanus faked an arm injury and kept a knife wrapped up in the bandages. When the opportunity presented itself, Stephanus gave Domitian the old stab in the groin. Domitian fought back and tried claw the eyes out of his killer but failed and died from multiple stab wounds. This was the glorious end to the Flavian Dynasty.

## Dot 10: The Five Good Emperors and the Antonine Dynasty (96–192)

Domitian's death signaled not only the end of the Flavian Dynasty but also the end of Suetonius's famous book *The Twelve Caesars*. For most of the next century, Rome would be governed by a series of emperors who came to power by a variety of means. This era includes one of the more remarkable men of the Roman Empire—the emperor/philosopher Marcus Aurelius, who tempered a life spent on military campaigns by writing aphorisms about life and thought. His son Commodus, of course, turned out to be more of the psychopath/megalomaniac type we've seen at the head of Rome since the time of Augustus. His actions would bring about the conclusion of the period of the Five Good Emperors, and he would end his father's short-lived dynasty.

Domitian's assassins made Nerva, a former consul, emperor because of his unique qualifications: he was elderly and had no children (and few allies). The plotters wanted someone they could control. He governed from

## CHAPTER TEN

96 to 98 and made Trajan his adopted son and heir. Then he died in the first month of 98.

Trajan became emperor upon Nerva's death and went to Rome in 99. The historian Pliny the Younger wrote and spoke about him in sycophantic terms. Trajan turned out to be one of the most militarily successful emperors and instituted a system of roads to hold together the empire. He created the first welfare system in the Western world, where money went to families with children. His relatively long reign concluded with his death in 117.

Then came Hadrian, who may or may not have been adopted by Trajan toward the end of the latter's life. Hadrian ensured his position in power by doling out a large sum of money to the troops and by making peace in the Mediterranean and in Parthia. Most important for European history, Hadrian divided Britain into northern and southern sections. The Scots in the north refused to be subdued, and so Hadrian commissioned a wall (appropriately called Hadrian's Wall) to be built across the center of the island of Britain between 122 and 132. This wall not only defined the edges of the Roman Empire but in time would also delineate between Britain and Scotland.

Hadrian also went to Jerusalem, renamed the city, and then sent his legions to crush a Jewish rebellion led by Simon Bar Kokhba, who claimed to be the Jewish messiah. After this, Hadrian expelled the Jews from Jerusalem. No Jewish state would again exist until after the Second World War.

Then Hadrian turned to solitude. He secured his succession by adopting Antonius Pius, and then required that Pius adopt Marcus Aurelius as his successor. Hadrian lived the life of a virtual hermit until he died in 138. Pius followed him as emperor, and his reign is noted for the continued expansion of the empire. He ordered that several revolts be crushed even though he never left Rome. When he died in 161, one of the most remarkable of the Romans, Marcus Aurelius, became Caesar.

## Dot 11: Marcus Aurelius

Already forty years of age when he became Caesar, Marcus Aurelius had already had just enough experience with politics (he'd served a one-year term as consul) to know he despised it. Aurelius preferred philosophy to politics and did not seem to relish the idea of being a Caesar. The Senate cajoled him into accepting the position, but Aurelius made them elevate his brother as co-Caesar.

Aurelius spent most of his time fighting wars. The focus of his military energy was on the Parthians, who had marched into the Middle East. Aurelius dispatched an army led by his brother to defeat the Parthians, but when the victorious troops returned, a Middle Eastern plague hitched a ride with them. In 166, plague not only scorched Rome but also sparked the thinking of a doctor named Galen, who had been a physician to the gladiators and whose work on disease and anatomy became the standard medical text in the West up until the Scientific Revolution.

The plague itself devastated Rome, lasting over three years and killing tens of thousands. Unhappy as Roman subjects, the barbarians whom the Romans had kept under control on the frontiers of Germany attacked Rome's borders. Aurelius's brother, meanwhile, died of mysterious seizures. This left Aurelius himself to defend the frontiers. He spent most of his remaining time as Caesar leading his troops to put out rebellions in Germany.

Aurelius earned a reputation as a frugal emperor who dealt kindly with people. He escaped the noise of the military camp by retreating into the inner halls of philosophy. During campaigns, he wrote *The Meditations of Marcus Aurelius*, which is primarily a collection of aphorisms about Stoic philosophy. It lives on as a classic in personal philosophy, ranking with Ashoka's pillars on Dhamma or the post-Soviet Czech leader Vaclav Havel's plays and philosophy as one of the few philosophical classics to be created by a person with political power.

Though he had more than a dozen children, only one, Commodus, survived to adulthood. Aurelius, in a hurry to get away from being the emperor, named Commodus as co-emperor when the boy was just fifteen. Aurelius died in the year 180 from an unknown ailment that caused him severe pain.

## Dot 12: Commodus

By the time Commodus became full emperor, he was nineteen and apparently tired of war. He negotiated peace treaties along the German frontier and then went back to Rome. Nobody with a blood tie to the emperor had inherited the position of Caesar since Domitian, as most of the emperors were adopted as a way of securing succession (a necessary occurrence, given that several of these emperors had no offspring). Aurelius showed no interest in finding a suitable candidate and so elevated his son. It turned out to be a bad choice.

Commodus fit the mold of Nero and Caligula. Once again, Rome became a playground where the sick fantasies of the Caesar could be acted out. Commodus built a harem with hundreds of boys and girls. His obsession with gladiatorial combat drove him to dress as a gladiator and "fight" in the arena itself. By now, however, the Romans knew how to deal with such a Caesar. In 192, some conspirators poisoned Commodus. He survived long enough to die from strangulation via the arms of a grappler.

## Dot 13: Assassinations, 192–193

Commodus left no clear heir, and in the year after his assassination no less than four men would claim to be Caesar. The Praetorian Guard, the bodyguards of the Caesar, decided who would rule. A man called Pertinax first rose to power, but he refused to dole out rewards to the guards and was executed by them in 193. Then Didius Julianus, a one-time consul, bribed the guards into making him emperor, but the Senate eventually disbarred him and the guards killed him. So, too, did Pescennius Niger die at the hands of his own guardians.

## Dot 14: House of Septimius Severus

In 193 BCE, Septimius Severus, a military commander stationed in Syria, turned his troops to Rome in order to restore order and put himself in power. The Senate, by then, had just removed Julianus, and Severus broke up the Praetorian Guard and defeated Niger, who'd taken power by force. The Senate, seeing the obvious, made Severus a Caesar.

He spent most of his campaign fighting, particularly in Britain, where he rebuilt parts of Hadrian's Wall. Like Aurelius, he died while out on campaign in the year 211. His descendants ruled Rome until 235, and most died messy deaths at the hands of conspirators. One of the descendants, Caracalla, issued a Constitution in 212 that granted citizenship to all of the freemen of the empire. The army officers killed him.

## Dot 15: The Soldier Emperors

In 235, the last of the House of Severus, a young man named Bassianius Alexianus, died while fighting in Persia. In 238, a general named Maximinus used force to gain power and then got the Senate to approve him. When he continued to campaign in Germany, the Senate revoked his title and Maximinus's soldiers executed him. For the next fifty years a succession of military figures took the title of emperor. Most died at the hands of their own soldiers or were executed by the Praetorian Guard. One of them, Quintillus, sat as emperor for only seventeen days before his soldiers killed him.

## Connecting the Dots

This bloody political situation increasingly mirrored the messy chaos found at the empire's frontiers. The barbarians seemed to be perpetually attacking Rome's borders. Rome's leaders, by necessity, had military backgrounds. The overreliance on the military, and the murderous tactics used to create and unseat emperors, destabilized Rome. The next era would belong to the tetrarchy, a political configuration that involved dividing Rome into four pieces. This is where the history of early Christianity connects with the history of Rome.

**CHAPTER ELEVEN**
# JUDAISM, CHRISTIANITY, AND CONSTANTINE

## Dot 1: Jewish Sources and Judaism

The history of early Judaism fits chronologically into the ancient era. However, to place it in the context of monotheistic history, it's better understood through its connections to Christianity and to Rome. Christianity grew from Judaism, but the first three hundred years of Christian history remain historically murky. Part of the confusion stems from the important—indeed, central—place that Christianity held in medieval Europe. Monks from that era who created the calendar divided history into the era "Before Christ" (BC) and the era following Jesus's birth (*Anno Domini* in Latin, meaning "Year of Our Lord").

Roman history from the era, however, seems to have paid little attention. We have no Roman records, for example, that detail the trial and execution of Jesus. And the Christians are not mentioned by other Romans for decades after the events detailed in the New Testament.

The Jewish holy book is called the Torah, or the Five Books of Moses. The Torah comprises the books of Genesis, Exodus, Leviticus, Numbers, and Deuteronomy. Christians include the Jewish Torah as the first part of the Old Testament. The Torah states that Abraham founded Judaism, but it is vague about the details of his life.

All three of the major monotheistic religions of Judaism, Christianity, and Islam trace their origins to Abraham. The Torah explains that Abraham's religious contribution was the concept of the covenant, which amounts to a deal with the Jewish God, named Yahweh. Believers pledged to follow the rules of Yahweh and, in return, Yahweh promised to reward his "chosen" people.

The Torah describes Yahweh as being jealous and not wanting his people to participate in the religious ceremonies of other gods or worship other deities. In a world where polytheism dominated, this notion of a singular god separated the early Jews from the rest of the ancient religious community.

Abraham had a son named Isaac; to test Abraham's faith, Yahweh commanded him to sacrifice Isaac. Abraham, the dutiful father, tied his son up and prepared to stab him to death, but before he brought the knife down, Abraham saw a ram tangled in a thicket. He understood that Yahweh intended this ram to be a replacement sacrifice for Isaac and that Yahweh had merely been testing the depth of his faith.

Isaac, in turn, begat two sons named Esau and Jacob. Jacob did a lot of begetting and had twelve sons, each of whom would become the founder of one of the twelve tribes of Israel. The second youngest of the twelve brothers went by the name of Joseph, and when Joseph received a many-colored coat from his father, this proved to be the tipping point for his already jealous siblings. They captured him and sold him into slavery. Joseph ended up in Egypt but, because of his powers as a fortune-teller, attained a high position at the court of the pharaoh (the Torah is not specific as to which historical pharaoh).

## Dot 2: Joseph to Moses

The Torah recounts how Joseph's brothers eventually came begging to Egypt, but they did not recognize their brother now that he had grown and gained a position of influence. Rather than taking revenge, Joseph worked it out so that his family could settle in Egypt, where they would stay for hundreds of years.

In later years, the Egyptians enslaved the Jews (known at this time as the Children of Israel or Hebrews) in the region of the Nile Delta. Moses enters the narrative here, but the Torah is vague on the chronology. Historians have trouble placing the life of Moses on a time line, but the Torah indicates that he would have lived sometime between 1220 and 1820 BCE.

The story of Moses contains many similarities to the story of Cyrus. The Old Testament tells of the pharaoh fearing that the Children of Israel were becoming too numerous. He thus ordered the killing of Israelite infants to stop the overpopulation. The mother of Moses placed her child in basket made of reeds and set him afloat on the Nile, where the pharaoh's daughter discovered the baby and then raised him.

Forty years later, Moses violently intervened when he saw a man whipping a Hebrew slave and, in the process, inadvertently killed the slaveholder. The Children of Israel later proclaimed Moses to be their leader. After ten plagues visited the Egyptians, Moses led his people out of Egypt. The book of Exodus ("the exit") tells the story of the pharaoh's men chasing Moses and his followers across the Red Sea (a mistranslation, according to many scholars, who have the Hebrews crossing the "Reed Sea," a shallow body of water where the pharaoh's men would have gotten stuck in the mud), with Yahweh parting the waters so they could cross. When the pharaoh and his men gave chase, Yahweh removed his hand and the walls of water crashed down upon the Egyptians.

Newly freed from Egypt, the Hebrews now wandered for forty years in the desert, looking for the Promised Land. A mysterious food called manna fell from the sky every morning, and the Hebrews largely survived upon it. The wandering Hebrews also made war on the pagans they encountered. The book of Deuteronomy is among the bloodiest texts of the ancient world, with Yahweh commanding his people to eradicate not only paganism but also every practitioner of pagan religions.

Along the way, Moses climbed Mt. Sinai, spoke with Yahweh, and brought down the Ten Commandments. The first of these, translated around two millennia later by the English, reads, "Thou shall have no other gods before me." This aggressive stance toward polytheism would, in time, remake the Western world and divide it culturally from the eastern regions where polytheism continued to reign.

The Promised Land, known as Canaan, remained elusive until, after four decades of wandering and occasional loss of faith, the Hebrews sighted this territory. Moses, who had angered Yahweh by taking personal credit for a miracle when the glory belonged to Yahweh, did not get to enter. Shortly thereafter Moses climbed Mt. Nebo (an impressive act for a

CHAPTER ELEVEN

man rumored to be one hundred and twenty years old), took a long look at the Holy Land, and then died. Yahweh disposed of the body.

## Dot 3: The Promised Land

At this point, the Children of Israel, now led by Joshua, entered Canaan. The Israelites divided the land and appointed Saul as Israel's first king. David (who slayed a giant named Goliath as a young man, and who sinned badly with a woman named Bathsheba while in power) became the second king after defeating Saul. Solomon followed David, his father, as king. Upon Solomon's death, the kingdom split, with the northern ten tribes taking the name of Israel and the southern two tribes being called Judah.

Strong powers surrounded Israel. In about 587–586 BCE, the Babylonians destroyed the great Temple. In Jewish history, this cataclysmic event is known as the first episode of the Diaspora, or dispersal. Many Israelites took the destruction of their temple as a sign of Yahweh's disfavor. They must have broken the covenant with Yahweh. A prophet named Ezekiel promised to restore the covenant and further promised that the temple would be rebuilt. The Jews (as they were now coming to be known) continued to worship in the absence of a temple, and the books of the Torah likely took full written shape during this era.

Then the Persians overthrew the Babylonians, and the Jews moved back into Israel and rebuilt the temple. A couple of hundred years later, Alexander the Great conquered the region. Jewish and Greek culture clashed in the region, with many of the Jews enjoying the lifestyle of the Greeks while others rebelled against Greek influence. When Antiochus, the Greek ruler, interfered with Jewish religious rituals, many Jews exploded in revolution.

Despite the revolt's failure, by 142 BCE Israel formed into her own state. In 63 BCE, Caesar's rival Pompey conquered the area and ended the Jewish state. Another one would not exist until 1948.

## Dot 4: The Jews Roam into Rome

Deprived of a homeland, many of the Jews moved to Rome but took pains to remain separate from the Roman population, lest their culture be diluted. In fact, most Jews lived in isolated enclaves in the city so as to remain apart. In 37 BCE, the Roman Senate appointed a Jew, Herod the Great, as king of Judea.

The Gospel of Matthew, written much later, details that Herod believed that a "messiah" or savior had been born in his kingdom. Jealousy drove him to order all of the children under the age of two to be murdered. We have no Roman records or contemporary accounts of these murders, but, for later Christians, the story of the persecution of an infant Jesus would make up a key part of the Christian religious message.

Although historians debate what Herod did and did not do, he almost certainly existed, as he is mentioned in several different contemporary documents. He died in 4 BCE, and the kingdom split into three pieces. Rome absorbed Judea, and in 26 CE Pontius Pilate became the governor of that region.

By now, the Jews appear as a besieged group who despised the Romans as just another in a long line of conquerors. However, the Jews could not stop fighting among themselves, and violence marred many of their religious festivals. One of the Jewish groups took the name of the Zealots, who were defined by their desire to make a war and create a new and independent Israel. Almost all of the Jewish sects hoped for a savior—likely a military leader who could carve out the new state.

## Dot 5: Christian Sources

Even the light of historical analysis does little to illuminate the murkiness surrounding early Christian history. No other religion contains so many different types of source material written or compiled across a vast span of time. The Bible as it is now known did not exist until nearly four hundred years after the life of Jesus, who appears as the central figure. When theologians finally did assemble the Bible, they chose only four of the "gospels" (from the Greek, meaning "good news") to include while omitting at least twenty other narratives, now known as the non-canonical gospels, of the life of Jesus. Archaeologists have turned up several of these documents in recent years, further complicating the picture of early Christianity.

The primary source books for Christianity consist of the three Synoptic (meaning, in Greek, "to see together") Gospels of Matthew, Mark, and Luke, as well as the Gospel of John (which used sources different

## CHAPTER ELEVEN

from those of the first three). Historians are unsure who wrote these gospels. Later theologians attributed authorial names to them. Almost certainly, Jesus and his followers would have spoken Aramaic, but the original gospels, which have disappeared, were all written in Greek. Most historians believe the Gospel of Mark to have been the first written, in about 60 CE (about thirty years after the trial and execution of Jesus, which this gospel records).

Mark contains no mention of the nativity (the story of the birth of Jesus in a stable). It does, however, detail part of the life of Jesus, beginning with his ministry at about the age of thirty and ending with his death by crucifixion and ensuing resurrection from the dead after three days. In the year 130 CE, a bishop named Papias attributed this gospel to a man named Mark mentioned in one of the letters of Peter.

Someone likely recorded the Gospel of John between the years 100 and 150. John differs considerably from the other gospels in that the narrative presents Jesus as a powerful and otherworldly figure. Historians are also unsure who wrote the Gospel of Luke, although religious tradition has it that the author was Luke, a friend of Paul, who would turn out to be the most consequential theologian in the faith. Most historians believe this gospel to have been written about the year 80 or 85. Luke adds the nativity scene, with Mary giving birth to Jesus in a stable and the three wise men making a visit.

Matthew may feature as one of the most important documents in Western history since it contains a passage by which the Catholic Church claims its authority. Matthew, likely written in 85 or 90 by an unknown Syrian Christian, has Jesus rising from the dead and telling his disciples to carry on his message. Those disciples constitute the earliest church, and their leader, Peter, was the first of the popes, according to church doctrine.

As mentioned earlier, at least twenty other gospels, including the Gospel of Thomas, the Gospel of Mary, the Gospel of Peter, and the newly found Gospel of Judas (among many others), existed for the first 250–300 years of Christian history. Different sects of Christians would have read these scrolls, but at that time no church, central theology, or clear book of religious texts existed. It would not be until much later, when Rome's history connected with Christian history, that Christianity would formalize.

When that linkage happened, the four most closely connected gospels of Mark, Luke, John, and Matthew all got added to the Jewish holy writings (including the Torah), along with Paul's letters (as well as letters written by other early Christian leaders) and the book of Revelation (written by a later prophet), and compiled into the Bible. This consists of the Jewish scriptures (known as the Old Testament) along with the twenty-seven books of the New Testament. The Bible is better understood as a collection of works than as a single book.

## Dot 6: The Story

According to Christian tradition, sometime between 4 and 6 BCE a baby named Yeshua ben Joseph, later known as Jesus, was born into a Jewish community. The gospels of the New Testament recount that Jesus found employment as a carpenter until about the age of thirty, when he began to teach.

Jesus preached a message that formed the foundations of Christian doctrine. He claimed to be a savior, or messiah. He preached that two versions of an afterlife existed—one where those who believed in his message would go, and another where those who disbelieved would go. The former has come to be known as Heaven and the latter as Hell, although Jesus referred to Hell as the "lake of fire." These concepts were well known in the ancient Middle East, as the conceptual framework of a world consisting of light and darkness had been developed and preached by the Persian Zoroaster long before.

Traditional Judaism placed no emphasis on either the afterlife or the potential conversion of non-Jews. Jesus added both concepts, as he preached to everyone. At the famous Sermon on the Mount, Jesus introduced a "love thy neighbor" philosophy that equated the giving of oneself to Christian practice. In Mark, he taught that he would be taken to Heaven but would return to usher in the "end times" (Apocalypse, from the Greek) and a day of judgment. Jesus disappointed many potential followers by making it clear that he did not intend to create a political kingdom on Earth, but rather a spiritual kingdom in the afterlife.

A summary of the arguments, meanings, and interpretations surrounding the trial and execution of Jesus would stray too far from the central narrative here. But the broad story depicted in the gospels is that the Roman governor Pontius Pilate eventually had Jesus seized, tried, and executed via crucifixion. Christians believe that after three days, Jesus rose

CHAPTER ELEVEN

from the dead. Matthew attributes several supernatural events to this, including the tearing of the Veil of the Temple, a cloth that separated the holiest inner part of the temple from the congregation. Matthew also relates that the tombs of many of the dead in Jerusalem opened, and the undead walked the streets in anticipation of the rise of Jesus.

Matthew likewise recounts that the corpse of Jesus had been placed in a tomb, but when Mary Magdalene and Jesus's other friends came to see his body, they instead encountered an angel. The frightened women ran away but then encountered the newly risen Jesus on the road to Galilee. At this point, Matthew indicates that Jesus bade his twelve disciples to go on preaching, thus establishing the church, and then ascended to Heaven from the Mount of Olives. The primary disciples who would carry on his message were Peter (considered by Catholics to be the first pope) and James, the presumed brother of Jesus.

## Dot 7: Paul

In 64, Rome caught fire. The wooden structures surrounding the Circus Maximus burned for six days and turned three of the fourteen sections of Rome into ash. At this time, twenty-six-year-old Nero reigned as Caesar and had to blame the fire on someone. The Jews appeared to be an easy target, but they had been supporters of Julius Caesar during the Roman civil war, and much of Nero's power rested on the memory of Julius. By this time, however, a new sect of Jews—the Christians—had formed.

At this point, a brief divergence into religious history becomes necessary. After the life of Jesus, a certain sect of the Jews believed that Jesus had been the messiah. They were called "Christians," meaning "followers of the savior" in Greek. Other Jews decided that Jesus was not the messiah and continued on with their traditions.

Nero saw that difference between the two groups and decided that the vulnerability of the Christians made them good targets for blame. According to Christian tradition, Nero took out his sadistic impulses on early Christian martyrs. They died by being dressed in animal skins and thrown among wild dogs; many others were crucified, and more died by being covered in pitch and set afire—thus lighting the streets of Rome.

One Jewish sect, the Pharisees, viewed the Christians as false prophets for their worship of Jesus. According the New Testament book of Acts, the

Pharisees stoned an early Christian named Stephen to death. One of the killers of Stephen went by the name of Saul (or Paul, as he is now known).

We know of Paul from two sources: his letters, which are defined by the groups he wrote them to, as in the case where he wrote to a group of Greek Christians living in Corinth, and from the book of Acts, which was written anonymously and almost certainly not by Paul. According to Acts, Paul traveled to Damascus in Syria sometime after the murder of Stephen, but on the way he heard a voice calling in Hebrew, "Saul, Saul, why are you persecuting me?" Blinding light from Heaven knocked Paul down, but he stood up a changed man.

Paul's own letters do not include anything so dramatic, but he does refer to a revelatory experience. Theologians often cite Paul's narrative as a conversion, but it is not clear that Paul converted to Christianity, as it was not entirely clear, at this point, what Christianity meant. Paul's modern biographer, A. N. Wilson, contends that Paul remained a Jew.

After this experience, Paul began to philosophize on the meaning of the crucifixion and molded a theology around this event. Paul theorized that once people accepted Jesus's message, they became equals in the eyes of God and eventually would become a new person in Heaven. Paul preached a gospel of otherworldly equality, but he did not speak out against slavery, as this might have proved dangerous in a Roman society that counted half of its inhabitants as slaves.

In Paul's mind, the body and the spirit remained severed. To Paul, sin was inherent in the flesh, and the body tried to pull one's spirit down into a carnal pit. He especially despised sex, seeing it as sinful. He viewed marriage as being for people who were too weak to remain celibate, but he stated that sexual contact within marriage was religiously permissible. He thought little of marriage but considered it a better alternative than eternal hellfire. Paul's vision of the body, so directly opposite that of the Greeks and Romans, later informed the church's decision to create a celibate class of priests.

Paul partially completed his theology about the same time that someone recorded the Gospel of Mark. And he used the Roman road system to begin preaching and winning converts. For the next 250 years, Paul's theology would spread throughout the empire but converted only a minority of Romans, maybe 10 percent, to Christianity. The particulars of Paul's death remain a mystery. His thinking and writing shaped the early

CHAPTER ELEVEN

Christian religion, and, as will now become apparent, early Christian religion shaped the late part of the Roman Empire.

## Dot 8: Diocletian

Christian history formed within the larger narrative of the Roman Empire. The Romans took relatively little notice of either Jesus or the small sect of his followers who taught and worshiped in the empire for the next few hundred years. Then, rather suddenly, in the fourth century, Christianity's place in Rome shifted upward.

Between 284 and 305, Diocletian governed the empire. At this time, four men had divided the empire into regions. By 300, Diocletian emerged as the main power, having risen to prominence through his impressive military service. The military had proclaimed him emperor of its own accord, as the Senate by now had only ornamental significance.

In 285, Diocletian elevated a comrade, Maximian, to the rank of Caesar while he himself took the higher title of Augustus. A year later, he made Maximian an Augustus as well, and each of the men chose a new Caesar. This divided the empire into four pieces, a governmental structure known as a tetrarchy.

An impressive emperor, Diocletian used his military experience and passion for the campaign to put down a series of revolts and to conquer greater territory. Like a lot of emperors, his ego got away from him. Diocletian fancied himself a god and expected that the myriad religious cults in Rome would all pray to him before engaging in their regular worship activities. Jews and Christians thought such an act violated the First Commandment ("Thou shall have no other gods before me") and refused. The Jews had permission to do this, but the Christians did not.

Here's where it gets weird: Diocletian's soothsayers claimed to be able to see the future in the intestines of slaughtered animals, an age-old practice known as augury. Christians opposed this ritual, seeing it as pagan (pre-Christian), and would often cross themselves right at the moment of sacrifice. The fortune-tellers told Diocletian that the actions of the Christians angered the gods, and the gods in turn interfered with the prophecies.

Diocletian believed the gods to be in control of every action, so he took the accusations of the soothsayers seriously and introduced a vicious persecution of the Christians. They were banned from public office, and if they refused to swear loyalty to the emperor, they could be tortured in inventive ways.

Edward Gibbon, the great Enlightenment-era historian of Rome, estimates that two thousand Christians died. Historians continue to debate the severity of Diocletian's persecution. Then, out of nowhere, Diocletian appears to have gotten bored with being emperor, and in 305 he abdicated to become a farmer. No other emperor of Rome ever willingly gave up the throne. The Romans, likely shocked, once again had to prepare for a civil war.

## Dot 9: Constantine—In This Sign, Conquer

Diocletian's title should have passed to a man named Severus, but an army leader named Constantine who'd made a reputation in Britain decided he should be able to seize power. In the meantime, Severus discovered, no doubt to his dismay, that one of the Caesars (named Maximian) had taken over most of his army with bribes. Severus soon found himself under house arrest and committed suicide.

This set up a dramatic battle between Constantine and Maximian. Constantine just happened to be married to Maximian's daughter, so this would be a family affair. Maximian initially tried to convince his daughter to kill her husband, but she didn't go for it. According to legend, Maximian decided to murder Constantine himself and sneaked into the man's bedroom at night. Maximian stabbed someone lying in Constantine's bed, but it was a eunuch (which meant he'd had other bad experiences with a knife) whom Constantine had planted there when his wife had alerted him to her father's plan.

At this point, Constantine dramatically emerged from behind some curtains in the room and had his father-in-law seized by guards, who then broke his neck. But Maximian had a son, Maxentius, who proclaimed himself emperor of Rome, where he enjoyed the support of the powerful Praetorian Guard. Constantine turned his army to Rome to fight his brother-in-law for mastery.

Constantine later claimed that on the day before the battle he looked into the sky and beheld an image of a giant *chi-rho* sign (a type of Greek cross) along with the phrase *In Hoc Signo Vinces*.

## CHAPTER ELEVEN

In this sign, *conquer*.

On the next day, October 28, 312, Maxentius opened the gates to Rome. His army came marching out to meet Constantine's. The winner of this battle would control Rome.

To get his army across the Tiber River, Maxentius had his men build a bridge of boats. When Constantine pushed Maxentius's army backward, the engineers who had built the bridge panicked and allowed the boats to float away so that Constantine couldn't get across the river to Rome. The action tossed Maxentius and his men into the water, and their heavy armor dragged them to the bottom. Someone from Constantine's army pulled Maxentius's body from the water, hacked off the head, and placed it on a pike.

Constantine and his men then stormed into Rome, their grisly trophy held high. Constantine now ruled.

## Dot 10: Council of Nicaea

Few people believe that Constantine actually saw a cross in the sky before his battle. More likely, he saw a chance to consolidate his power and was interested, as at least one Egyptian ruler (Akhenaton) before him had been, in uniting his people under the belief in a single god. The ten-cent word describing this concept, *Caesaropapism*, would in time become known by the variation of "the divine right of kings." Constantine believed in the concept of "one god and one king," the notion being that monotheism provided a better fit for a monarchy than did the messy pantheon of gods that came with polytheism. Constantine quickly issued the Edict of Milan, which lifted any constrictions on Christian practice.

A major problem now confronted Constantine: he wanted to elevate Christianity to a privileged place in Rome's society, but the Christians were so fractured and quarrelsome that they were not much better than the polytheists. At this time, the primary question dividing the Christians involved the divinity of Jesus. Was he a god or was he not? One early Christian theologian, named Arius, taught that Jesus was the son of God, not God himself, and therefore not quite divine. Other Christians disagreed, believing that God and Jesus had to be the same since Jesus could not occupy a secondary place in Christian theology.

In the year 324 Constantine defeated his final rival for power. The next year he called a group of three hundred bishops together at his lakeside dwelling at the city of Nicaea. The objective he put before them was simple: create a theology.

They argued. Eventually, the date for Easter was resolved. Then they dealt with Arius's assertion about the divinity of Jesus. When the bishops voted, Arianism (as it was known) lost. The council instead adopted a theology called the Nicene Creed, which would become the centerpiece of Catholic teaching. The Nicene Creed taught that Jesus was "homousion" instead of "homoiousion," which meant he was the same as God rather than similar.

Arius believed this position to be nonsense. How can something be the same as something else, yet also be referred to as something different? He did not see that the Nicene Creed was not meant to be understood logically; instead, the church expected believers to take the concept purely on faith. Arius and his followers lost not only the vote over theology but also their lives. Shortly after the council, just before a supper where Arius was supposed to be reconciled with his fellow Christians, he became ill. When stomach pains caused him to rush to a public privy, his bowels fell out. Many of his enemies saw this as a punishment from God, but more likely someone had poisoned him. Shortly thereafter, three thousand of his followers were slaughtered.

Soon enough, far in the east, the Huns would rise to power and chase various tribal peoples into Western Europe. These refugees would overwhelm Rome but not the church.

## Connecting the Dots: Rome and Christianity

Constantine ranks as one of history's most important human beings. Not only did he end the persecution of Christians by invoking the Edict of Milan, but he also elevated Christianity more or less to the official religion of the Roman Empire. In doing so, he combined pagan Roman religious practices with Christian practices. Thus, the traditional Roman holiday of Saturnalia became the holiday of Christmas. Although Christians initially kept the Jewish Sabbath on Saturday, at some point very early on they began to worship on the day after Saturday, which was called "Sunday" by

## CHAPTER ELEVEN

the non-Christian Romans. Constantine made Sunday a holiday recognized by the Roman state.

Constantine also moved the capital east to the shores of the Black Sea in modern Turkey. Originally known as Byzantium, the city that Constantine founded as a co-capital of the Roman Empire would in time be named after him: Constantinople. Eventually, the two sections of the empire grew apart, and that narrative will be addressed in volume II.

As the narrative of volume I concludes, we leave the Han Dynasty at its peak, India under the reign of Ashoka, and Rome as a newly Christian empire. Volume II will focus on the collapse of all three of these powerful early political structures. Two new powers will emerge from the chaos to dominate the seventh, eighth, and ninth centuries: Islam and the Tang Dynasty, founded at roughly the same time. Both religion and empire will, once again, connect many of the dots of Eurasian civilization.

# APPENDIX

## Common Core and Other Literacy Standards

New literacy standards, including Common Core and the state-level variations that politics has forced it to assume, will benefit students. These new educational philosophies are based on decades of solid research into classroom practice and should be taken seriously by teachers. The new Common Core philosophy, which places emphasis on a student's ability to read academic text, create a thesis, and support that thesis with textual evidence, will give teachers a much-needed common set of skills to be taught.

The problem comes when the entire educational bureaucracy, including the myriad of testing and textbook-and-workbook companies, decides that the Common Core requires their expertise and that (not incidentally) they should be the ones to make a nice profit from the implementation of the standards. In this respect, the Common Core shift looks a lot like all of the other educational fads that sweep through schools every few years, leaving teachers frustrated and parents bewildered.

These "fads" are sometimes depicted as a by-product of problems inherent within educational research, in the sense that conflicting findings (which are inevitable, given the size and complexity of the research samples) leads to a series of ever-changing initiatives. Common Core should be seen for what it is: a sound philosophy to be adopted by teachers when they are engaged in the business of synthesizing educational philosophy with content for the purpose of classroom implementation.

APPENDIX

I will defend the concept of a mandated Common Core test for the same reason that I will defend the Advanced Placement programs. (I have taught Advanced Placement world history for a number of years.) The idea of a class that culminates in a rigorous test is, in general, a good one, provided that the test is good. The Advanced Placement test for world history is a good one, and the new Common Core exams are as well.

Let me make these points: A good test—that is, a test that aligns with educational best practices—can positively alter curricula. Teachers are paid with tax dollars and should not complain when asked to be held accountable by the community. This being said, it's relatively cheap to create good tests (I've created several for this curriculum), and it's not clear why millions or billions of dollars need to flow into the coffers of educational conglomerates for the purpose of test creation.

Classroom educators certainly do not need to be forced to implement "teacher-proof" classroom materials that are guaranteed to meet the new literacy standards. Teachers can create these materials for their own classrooms and, in the process of creation, develop their own content-area knowledge and intimacy with the curriculum, which is necessary to enhance the learning experience of students.

Educational methodology really is not that complicated. Students do not need expensive textbook-and-workbook materials or new technologies. A recent book, *Academically Adrift: Limited Learning on College Campuses*, presented findings that should have brought about an entire overhaul of the American educational system. The authors, Richard Arum and Josipa Roksa, used the College Learning Assessment, a Common Core–style exam that measures not a student's content-area knowledge but his or her critical thinking skills, to measure the cognitive progress of college students in their first two years.

They found that "with a large sample of more than 2,300 students, we observe no statistically significant gains in crucial thinking, complex reasoning, and writing skills for at least 45 percent of the students in our study" (p. 36). The authors further found that students who studied primarily in groups and who took courses with light reading and writing loads did not generally improve their cognitive skills. The one thing consistent among students who did improve their cognitive skills was that they took classes that required at least fifty pages of reading a week and the writing of at least one twenty-page paper. They tended to study alone.

APPENDIX

If the research is so clear about what helps students learn, then why is the process of educating students presented as such a complicated mess? Here's the problem with announcing to the world that students improve their cognitive functioning when they (a) have a great teacher, (b) read a lot, and (c) write a lot: It looks too simple. It looks too inexpensive. It looks like it can be done by investing more in teacher education and making sure that every student gets a library card, a pad of paper, and a pencil.

Society has problems; students come to school with a myriad of personal calamities that are not so easy to tackle, but those issues go beyond the scope of this book. Let's stick narrowly here with the issue of increasing a student's cognitive skills, which is the purpose of school. Students who live in poverty and students who live in wealth both need great teachers, and they need to read and write a lot.

## How to Use This Curriculum

First of all, another teacher cannot fully implement my curriculum or anyone else's. A teacher should create her own curriculum. The act of doing so will enhance her content-area knowledge and her cognitive skills, both of which have been shown to correlate with improved student achievement. That being said, creating a 180-day curriculum is an exhausting process that can take many years. A teacher might want to make use of this curriculum in the meantime.

Part of the Common Core philosophy is that content transmission should take place primarily through reading. Lectures and activities (even group activities) are essential parts of education, but reading is the core. The problem with textbooks is that, as James Loewen has indicated, they are designed to be *bought*, not read. Why doesn't anyone ever read a textbook unless forced to for class credit?

I have read widely on a variety of topics myself and have never felt compelled to pick up a textbook. This is because textbooks lack a narrative; they just dump information between two covers without connecting it to a compelling story. If neuroscience has made any consistent finding, it is that people retain information only when it is placed in a narrative. History, more than any other subject, requires narrative. This curriculum is designed to tell a story and to raise a student's level of reading comprehension during the process.

APPENDIX

Some assessments are included here as examples, and I will include others in the future volumes, but I encourage teachers to create their own. I have deliberately not included the entire assessment piece of the curriculum because I don't want to give the impression that it can be used as is by another teacher. Teachers will have to engage with the work by creating assignments and lesson plans. Toward that end, the assessments are listed in the next section and a greater level of description will be included there.

Before addressing the assessments, I will point out that this curriculum (and the philosophy of which it is a product) is intended for secondary teachers. Teachers of grades 7–12 will likely find this useful, and there are applications for the collegiate level, which badly needs to define teaching as a field, lest the research model divert them even further from their mission of educating students. I have nothing of value to say to elementary teachers except "thank you."

## Assessments

As stated earlier, teachers should not be afraid of tests. Tests can be crucial for targeting the areas where students need improvement. Furthermore, teachers should embrace state-mandated tests (provided they are in alignment with educational theory) in no small part because they give teachers an excuse to push students.

It might surprise the public, but will not surprise teachers, that parents oftentimes put pressure on school districts to make classes less rigorous. I am sometimes still shocked that a significant minority of parents harbor the notion that it's my job not to teach a student anything, but simply to provide affirmation that the student already knows how to do something. Anything beyond handing students information and then asking them to spit it back on a test is considered, somehow, "unfair" by people with this mindset.

Federally mandated tests can have the effect of mandating a high level of rigor. This allows for teachers to push students under the auspice of making sure that students are prepared for their assessments. This is a good solution to the grade-inflation problem and gives teachers a chance to break out of the "customer service" model of education, described and decried in the previously mentioned book *Academically Adrift*, and also in *Excellent Sheep: The Miseducation of the American Elite* by William Deresiewicz, that has proved to be so harmful at the secondary and collegiate level.

This curriculum is designed to have students prepare for a Common Core–style final that requires a high level of reading comprehension, the ability to recognize and decide between arguments, and, most important, the ability to develop and analyze analogies. If this looks like something that is too difficult for students, then please recognize that nothing else qualifies as thinking.

Giving students a study guide and then having them fill in blanks based on the exact content in the guide might allow a teacher to fill in a gradebook, but it does nothing to actually test cognitive skills. It does not give the instructor or the students a skill set to develop.

Creating questions that go along with the reading is a crucial component of the new literacy standards. No examples of reading questions are included here, as each teacher will need to generate her own questions. As a broad rule, however, teachers should require that the answers to each question include "textual evidence," or quotes from the text.

Now here's the semi-revolutionary part: the students will do most of the reading in class. With all of the digital distractions now available to young people, one of the most valuable things I can do as a teacher is control the environment so they can actually sit and read. Reading is an activity too important to be assigned as an outside-the-class activity. Teachers sometimes like to compare themselves to doctors as a way to argue against accountability standards. The argument includes some variation of "doctors can prescribe a medication or treatment but can't be held accountable if the patient does not follow through."

This analogy does not fit. Teachers see their patients five days a week and can control whether they take their prescriptions. I want students reading, and so I'm going to enforce that objective by bringing this important activity inside the classroom. If a doctor had the opportunity to see a patient every day for forty-five minutes and could control the patient's actions, he would probably put the guy on a treadmill.

So class generally begins with students having twenty to twenty-five minutes to read and answer questions. After that, the class activities take

## APPENDIX

place. This might be a group discussion followed by a teacher-led Q&A session, a lecture, or a group activity. These activities enhance the content-area knowledge of students and bring to class an important element of variety. It's my contention that the content of world history is interesting enough to keep students hooked, and the relatively short sections of "dots" allow for students to engage with content in manageable chunks.

Students do not all read at the same pace, obviously. In order to deal with this fundamental problem, I typically require that four or five questions for the day be completed during the reading time. That's about as much as the best readers can handle. If someone finishes, I post an "if you finish" activity on the board, something that is as ever-present as the day's date. This discourages students from rushing through their work and prevents me from ever having to hear those two words, favored by students all over the world, that demonstrate a total misunderstanding of the purpose of education. I speak, of course, of the phrase "I'm done."

What students do not finish, they will have to complete the questions at home. The digital version of this curriculum is posted online, and if I encounter a student without a home computer, then I make a hardcopy of the materials available. Students who read at a slower pace still have to finish the work, but they can do so in a lower-pressure home environment. If students don't complete it at home, then at least they gained some benefit from the in-class work.

One of the valid criticisms of the Common Core philosophy and its variations is that it degrades the importance of content. Part of the reason that content is largely absent from the standards has to do with the toxin of controversy, particularly as it pertains to the standards for U.S. history. Common Core therefore focuses on reading comprehension skills while allowing states or districts to decide what content to teach those skills with. This philosophy has been formed with a rather narrow understanding of content and how it can be assessed.

Somehow, the concept of content-area testing has been intertwined with recall exams that use that old trifecta of educational mediocrity: the multiple-choice, fill-in-the-blank, and matching-of-terms format. Content can be tested in more cognitively challenging ways. This is the idea behind Fix-This-Scenario quizzes. In these assessments, students are given a scenario that includes eight mistakes and are challenged to find three of those mistakes and correct them with the right content. This tests what students have mastered rather than what students recognize from a study guide.

In the papers I have written on philosophy and theoretical physics, and also in my book *Novum Organum II*, I have argued extensively about the importance of analogy for deep thinking. Content fuels analogy and analogy is, to borrow from the title of Douglas Hofstadter and Emmanuel Sander's latest book, "the fuel and fire of thinking." The neuroscientist Daniel Willingham has written that it's a fallacy to think that creative thought exists separate from content-area mastery. One cannot *think* without having some content to *think about*. The more that someone knows about a topic, the more detailed the analogy one can create between two disparate topics.

One way, therefore, to test student content-area knowledge is to require the development of analogies between the content being studied and something that has been previously studied. Students must then apply "recall" knowledge to a new situation. This is how content can be tested through deep cognitive functions.

Analogy rescues the humanities and should be added to the Common Core philosophy as a way of enhancing the credentials of the philosophy. No controversy need accompany this change, as the use of content for the creation of analogies does not require any agreed-upon set standards of what should or should not be taught. Instead, it sets a standard for what students should be able to do no matter what type of content has been taught.

The goal for the semester is to have students ready to read and comprehend academic text, derive a deep concept from the reading, and apply that knowledge to another, potentially analogous situation. Since these are the assessments, the curriculum is designed to inculcate certain skills in the students.

This is the well-known concept of "backward planning." Another major concept in education involves teaching student "transfer" skills—that is, skills taught in a lesson that can be applied elsewhere. The assessment included in this volume is one that appeared in *Teaching Genius*, and it is intended as a first-quarter test, one linked to a more comprehensive exam that will be included in volume II.

Critical thinking and reading skills can be taught through practice in the same way that a musician learns to play the violin. Students of the

# APPENDIX

violin do not fill out worksheets about how to play the violin and then try to cram facts in their head the night before a recital. They practice daily, and when the recital occurs they play the same music they have been working on. A good class should operate under the same principles in the sense that students should be asked to perform the same skills they have been working on daily.

It is hard, but, to reiterate an earlier point, nothing else actually constitutes thought. Nothing else is acceptable.

## Sample End-of-Quarter Assessment

### Quote I

In Paul Cartledge's book *The Spartans*, a Spartan defeat during the Peloponnesian War is detailed:

> [I]n the seventh year of the War, in 425.... Incredible news reached the outside world of an extraordinary happening on Sphacteria, a small island just off the south-west coast of Messenia and within Sparta's home territory. A 400 strong force of Spartan and Perioecic hoplites, including 120 of the Homoioi or Peers, had surrendered there following a twelve-week blockade by Athenian forces aided by descendants of former Messenian Helots. This event shook the Greek world. It simply was not supposed to happen. For it contradicted absolutely the Spartan myth, as laid down and exemplified most famously at Thermopylae, the myth of Never Surrender ...
>
> To the Greeks as a whole, and to the Spartans in particular, it was inconceivable that 120 products of the Agoge education system would surrender after a mere eighty days of privation, thirst and hunger.
>
> When questioned about that very fact, one of the prisoners in Athens is said to have given as his reason for surrendering that he hadn't been involved in a fair fight, man to man. He hadn't been fighting against true men in regular warfare using masculine weapons. Instead, he had been brought low by what he called the enemies' "spindles," which he claimed were incapable of distinguishing a true warrior from a born coward. The reference of "spindles," Thucydides explains, was to arrows—ignoble, cowardly, long-distance weapons, typically womanish. (p. 35)

# APPENDIX

Quote II

In Alfred Crosby's *Throwing Fire: Projectile Technology through History*, the author quotes:

> A single one of us can defeat your whole army. If you do not believe it, you may try, only please order your army to stop shooting with firearms. (An unnamed Mamluk emir, prisoner to Selim the Grim, Ottoman Sultan, after the battle of Marjdabik, 1516)

Quote III

> Victory did not come to the one who played by the rules; it came to the one who made the rules and imposed them on the enemy. (Jack Weatherford, p. 56)

**Assigned Essay:** Compare Quotes I and II. The Spartans and the Arabs, separated by two thousand years, are lamenting the same problem. Once you understand the quotes, explain what Dr. Weatherford means in Quote III.

World History    Name _____

                                         Date _____ Pd ___

## World History Final Exam Essay Rubric Part II

Content:

___ **12 Content:** (Includes textual evidence from Quote I)
   —12–11 Includes textual evidence and analysis
   —10–9 Includes some analysis using textual evidence
   —8–7 Includes little analysis and/or little use of textual evidence
   —5–6 Includes little analysis and no use of textual evidence

___ **12 Content:** (Includes textual evidence from Quote II)
   —12–11 Includes textual evidence and analysis
   —10–9 Includes some analysis using textual evidence
   —8–7 Includes little analysis and/or little use of textual evidence
   —5–6 Includes little analysis and no use of textual evidence

APPENDIX

___ 12 **Content:** (Includes textual evidence from Quote III)
—12–11 Includes textual evidence and analysis
—10–9 Includes some analysis using textual evidence
—8–7 Includes little analysis and/or little use of textual evidence
—5–6 Includes little analysis and no use of textual evidence

Conventions:

___ 12 **Analysis Using a Historical Analogy:**
—12–11 Analogy is relevant, detailed, and aids in analysis
—10–9 Analogy is somewhat detailed and moderately aids in analysis
—8–7 Analogy is too shallow or does not aid in analysis

___ 12 **Thesis Statement:** (1 point for underlined thesis statement)
—12 Quality one-sentence thesis statement that specifically addresses the essay question
—11 Good one-sentence thesis statement but lacks focus
—10 One-sentence thesis statement is evident but needs work in addressing the essay question
—9 Thesis statement is attempted but does not address the essay question
—8 Thesis statement is not apparent

___ 12 **Overall Clarity and Structure:**
—12–11 The essay's structure is clear and sequential
—10–9 The essay's structure is somewhat clear and sequential
—8–7 The essay's structure lacks clarity and sequence

_____/72 ____ **Grade**

**Comments:**

# REFERENCES

Arum, Richard, and Josipa Roksa. (2011). *Academically Adrift: Limited Learning on College Campuses.* Chicago: University of Chicago Press.
Bauer, Susan Wise. (2007). *The History of the Ancient World: From the Earliest Accounts to the Fall of Rome.* New York: W. W. Norton.
Burke, James. (2007). *Connections: From Ptolemy's Astrolabe to the Discovery of Electricity: How Inventions are Linked—And How They Cause Change Throughout History.* New York: Simon & Schuster.
Cantor, Norman F. (2001). *In the Wake of the Plague: The Black Death and the World It Made.* New York: Perennial.
Cartledge, Paul. (2003). *The Spartans: The World of the Warrior-Heroes of Ancient Greece.* New York: Overlook Press.
Chen, Ingfei. (May 2006). Born to Run. *Discover.* Retrieved from http://discovermagazine.com/2006/may/tramps-like-us.
Cohen, Marc S., Patricia Curd, and C. D. C. Reeve. (2000). *Readings in Ancient Greek Philosophy: From Thales to Aristotle.* 2nd ed. Cambridge, MA: Hackett.
Collins, Michael, ed. (2012). *The Illustrated Bible: Story by Story.* London: DK Press.
Crosby, Alfred W. (2002). *Throwing Fire: Projectile Technology through History.* Cambridge: Cambridge University Press.
Deresiewicz, William. (2014). *Excellent Sheep: The Miseducation of the American Elite and the Way to a Meaningful Life.* New York: Free Press.
Diamond, Jared. (1992). *The Third Chimpanzee: The Evolution and Future of the Human Animal.* New York: Harper Perennial.
Diamond, Jared. (1999). *Guns, Germs, and Steel: The Fates of Human Societies.* New York: W. W. Norton.

REFERENCES

Diamond, Jared. (September 2005). The Shape of Africa. *National Geographic.* Retrieved from http://ngm.nationalgeographic.com/ngm/0509/resources_geo2.html.
Fenby, Jonathan. (2007). *China's Imperial Dynasties: 1600 BC–AD 1912.* New York: Metro.
Gibbon, Edward. (2003). *The Decline and Fall of the Roman Empire.* New York: Modern Library Classics. (Original work published in 1776.)
Grant, R. G. (2010). *Commanders: History's Greatest Military Leaders.* London: DK Press.
Herodotus. (2003). *The Histories.* Translated by Aubrey De Sélincourt, revised with introduction and notes by John Marincola. New York: Penguin Books.
Hofstadter, Douglas, and Emmanuel Sander. (2013). *Surfaces and Essences: Analogy as the Fuel and Fire of Thinking.* New York: Basic Books.
Homer. (1950). *The Iliad of Homer: The Wrath of Achilles.* Translated by I. A. Richards. New York: W. W. Norton.
Homer. (2012). *The Odyssey.* Retold by Gillian Cross. Somerville, MA: Candlewick Press.
Jones, Terry. (2006). *The Story of One.* PBS Home Video.
Kagan, Donald. (2003). *Peloponnesian War.* New York: Viking.
Keay, John. (2000). *India: A History.* New York: Grove Press.
Keay, John. (2009). *China: A History.* New York: Basic Books.
Kirsch, Jonathan. (2004). *God Against the Gods: The History of the War Between Monotheism and Polytheism.* New York: Viking.
MacCulloch, Diarmaid. (2009). *Christianity: The First Three Thousand Years.* New York: Viking.
Matyszak, Philip. (2003). *Chronicle of the Roman Republic: The Rulers of Ancient Rome from Romulus to Augustus.* London: Thames & Hudson.
McCarthy, Cormac. (1985). *Blood Meridian, or the Evening Redness in the West.* New York: Vintage International.
Montefiore, Simon Sebag. (2011). *Jerusalem: The Biography.* New York: Alfred A. Knopf.
Moynahan, Brian. (2002). *God's Bestseller: William Tyndale, Thomas More, and the Writing of the English Bible—A Story of Martyrdom and Betrayal.* New York: St. Martin's Press.
Nicolson, Adam. (2003). *God's Secretaries: The Making of the King James Bible.* New York: HarperCollins.
Pagden, Anthony. (2008). *Worlds at War: The 2,500 Year Struggle Between East and West.* New York: Random House.
Plutarch. (1965). *The Makers of Rome.* Translated by Ian Scott-Kilvert. New York: Penguin Classics.

# REFERENCES

Plutarch. (1993). *Plutarch's Lives*. Translated by John Dryden, revised by Arthur Hugh Clough. Norwalk, CT: Easton Press. (Originally edited by Charles W. Eliot in 1909 as part of the Harvard Classics.)

Reader, John. (1997). *Africa: A Biography of the Continent*. New York: Vantage Press.

Roberts, J. M., and O. A. Westad. (2013). *The History of the World*. 6th ed. Oxford: Oxford University Press.

Russell, Bertrand. (1945). *A History of Western Philosophy*. New York: Simon & Schuster.

Somner, Michael. (2010). *The Complete Roman Emperor: Imperial Life at Court and On Campaign*. London: Thames & Hudson.

Stephenson, Paul. (2009). *Constantine: Roman Emperor, Christian Victor*. New York: Overlook Press.

Stone, I. F. (1989). *The Trial of Socrates*. New York: Anchor Books.

Stott, Rebecca. (2012). *Darwin's Ghosts: The Secret History of Evolution*. New York: Spiegel & Grau.

Suetonius. (1957). *The Twelve Caesars*. Translated by Robert Graves. New York: Penguin Classics. (Revised and edited in 1979 by Michael Grant.)

Temple, Robert. (2007). *The Genius of China: 3,000 Years of Science, Discovery, and Invention*. London: Andre Deutsch.

Thucydides. (1996). *The Landmark Thucydides: A Comprehensive Guide to the Peloponnesian War*. Edited by Robert B. Strassler, translated by Victor Davis Hanson. New York: Simon & Schuster.

Vandiver, Elizabeth. (1999). *The Iliad of Homer: Course Guidebook*. Chantilly, VA: The Great Courses.

Wheeler, P. E. (May 1988). Stand Tall and Stay Cool. *New Scientist* (London) 118: 62–65.

Willingham, Daniel T. (2009). *Why Don't Students Like School? A Cognitive Scientist Answers Questions about How the Mind Works and What It Means for the Classroom*. New York: Jossey-Bass.

Wilson, A. N. (1992). *Jesus: A Life*. New York: W. W. Norton.

Wilson, A. N. (1997). *Paul: The Mind of the Apostle*. New York: W. W. Norton.

# ABOUT THE AUTHOR

**Chris Edwards** teaches world history and Advanced Placement world history at Fishers High School in central Indiana, and he is the author of both *Teaching Genius: Redefining Education with Lessons from Science and Philosophy* (2012) and *Novum Organum II: Going Beyond the Scientific Research Model* (2014). He writes on topics as varied as philosophy, theoretical physics, law, logic, and psychology for the science and philosophy journals *Skeptic and Free Inquiry*, and his scholarship and teaching methodology have been published in journals produced by both the National Council for History Education and the National Council for Social Studies. He also directs a professional development grant for math and science teachers that is funded by the Indianapolis-based Scientech Foundation.

www.ingramcontent.com/pod-product-compliance
Lightning Source LLC
Chambersburg PA
CBHW030140240426
43672CB00005B/201